Essex County Council

Many libraries in Essex
have videos for loan —

enquire at your local library
for details

HAS THE COUNTDOWN BEGUN?

HAS THE COUNTDOWN BEGUN?

Through Darkness to Enlightenment

Paco Rabanne

Translated from the French

SOUVENIR PRESS

Copyright © 1993 by Paco Rabanne
Translation by Michael Heron Copyright © 1994 by Souvenir Press

The right of Paco Rabanne to be identified as author of this
work has been asserted by him in accordance with the
Copyright, Designs and Patents Act 1988.

First published 1993 as *La Fin des Temps*
by Michel Lafon, Paris, France

English edition first published 1994 by
Souvenir Press Ltd
43 Great Russell Street, London WC1B 3PA
and simultaneously in Canada

ISBN 0 285 63190 X

Photoset by Rowland Phototypesetting Ltd,
Bury St Edmunds, Suffolk

Printed in Great Britain by
Mackays of Chatham PLC Chatham, Kent

Contents

Acknowledgements

My first book, *Trajectoire*, gave me the great pleasure of working as a team with Huguette Maure and Olivier de Broca.

I thank them for this new book, written with due regard for my inspiration, worked on with perseverance and love.

And I hope that all three of us have followed this pathway to enlightenment in all humility . . .

A few words by way of thanks ...
and of warning

First of all I must thank the numerous readers of my
first book who took the trouble to write to me to say
that they shared my convictions and that they had
experienced similar or even more extraordinary spiritual revelations and adventures. It is physically
impossible for me to answer all of them, but it is
reassuring (for them and for me) to discover that an
'individual' vision of the world no longer brands us
as lunatics or freaks at a fair. Perhaps my book will
have helped to shake the foundations of a scepticism
that is so often harmful to the quest for truth. Doubt
masquerading as dogma has the serious disadvan-
tage of inhibiting progress. Today more than ever we
should all try to be 'initiates': we should all embark
on the quest for Knowledge. It gives me great satisfac-
tion, therefore, to learn from some of the letters that
I have been able to point out some new avenues of
exploration!

Despite my theme of hope and inquiry, I did not
allow myself the luxury of lulling the reader into a
feeling of smug optimism, so the pages I devoted to
the Apocalypse and its first manifestations provoked
a huge response. Some people criticised me for paint-
ing too black a picture of the future. At the conferences where I subsequently had occasion to speak
about the end of Time, I kept seeing the frightened
faces (and the sceptical looks) of those to whom I had
announced out of the blue the terrible fate hanging
over our heads. So much so that I finally decided to
open my speeches, as I do here, with a warning:
'Fasten your seat-belts, hold on tight, for you're in
danger of getting it full in the face.'

It has never been easy to play Cassandra. Sounding the alarm is regarded as a breach of etiquette. In antiquity, people went so far as to kill the bearers of bad news. Today, in spite of the warning lights that are flashing red all over the place, there are many who simply prefer to keep wearing their reassuring blinkers. No doubt they imagine they will be all right if they ignore what is going on around them.

Nevertheless, during the last few months I have noticed that my 'alarmist' remarks have been getting a different reception. People seem to be more receptive to what I have to say; they listen to me more attentively than before. Most of the letters I receive have even criticised me for not going far enough! Those listeners (or readers) would like me to toughen up my warnings, in the hope perhaps of modifying the suicidal route mankind is taking.

This new attitude results from a conviction that everybody has now been forced to accept: 'Things cannot go on like this', we hear people saying wherever we go. A mood of extraordinary tension is gripping a world confronted by a mass of problems that are apparently insoluble and on the increase: the population explosion, the manifold and disastrous effects of pollution, disturbing developments in genetics, ethnic and urban violence, mental confusion . . . Everyone has a vague feeling that we have badly mishandled our dealings with each other and with Nature. Like others in the past, our civilisation has reached breaking point.

'Things cannot go on like this . . .' If that's true, what is going to happen?

Many prophetic books can enlighten us about the disasters to come. Surely it is always better to know—all the more so as we may hope to find in these prophecies the guidance that could help us to get out of the rut.

My last book was primarily an autobiography. This one is undoubtedly more ambitious: its theme is the future of mankind. In a way, the first book marked the end of the age of Pisces (an age of inner, personal quest); the second is intended to be the book of transition towards the age of Aquarius, which will be under the sign of fraternity and collective solidarity.

Unfortunately, this transition is likely to happen in the most appalling manner if we do not mend our ways.

It is not my intention to inspire terror, but to expose the threats that menace our future. For the rest, as the Old Testament says: 'He that heareth, let him hear; and he that forbeareth, let him forbear!'

Chapter 1

EMERGENCY!

*Write the things which thou hast seen and
the things which are, and the things
which shall be hereafter.*

Revelation

Write the things which I have seen . . . That advice
seems easy enough to follow, although I have not
always taken it. Whenever I was writing in the past,
I used to keep something back. Why? The first reason
may seem rather dubious, but it is real enough to
me. I was afraid of hearing what the sceptics, or even
worse, the scoffers, would have to say about me. For
I have often noticed that, whether they are in the
public eye or not, people expose themselves to ridicule as soon as they pluck up the courage to air their
innermost beliefs in public—especially when these
are based more on personal feelings than on logical
reasoning, more on forebodings than on tangible
proof.

Yet today we are witnessing the despotic reign of
absolute reason, glorified by the Age of Enlightenment and caricatured by the positivism of the Industrial Revolution, now beginning to totter on its
foundations. The often disastrous consequences (on
the ecological and human level) of our worship of
sacrosanct 'progress' are gradually instilling a little
more humility into human understanding. We find,
for example, that in their recent Olympian pronouncements, our 'rational' scientists have simply
rediscovered the message that the choir of mystics

has been repeating down the ages—spirituality takes absolute precedence over materialism.

It was undoubtedly this favourable climate of opinion that persuaded me to reveal my secrets for the first time. I felt that the moment had come and that I would not instantly be certified as a raving madman, without being given a hearing. As for the term 'illuminato' that is sometimes applied to me, I am quite willing to accept it. I would always rather be 'alight' than extinguished.

Isn't it better to embark on a quest for the truth (even if it turns out to be one's own personal truth in the end) than to be condemned to remain imprisoned forever within a straitjacket of prejudices that have not even the merit of ensuring our moral and spiritual comfort? Why not put one's trust in a consistent, ordered world, since believing it to be without purpose condemns us to inevitable despair?

That is why I began my first book by declaring my belief in reincarnation, a belief according to which our present existence is only one link in the chain of lives forming the 'trajectory' of our inner being. I revealed the signs and visions that had fostered this conviction from my earliest days and how the recollections of my former lives were imprinted on my memory. Then I spoke of the 'gifts' of clairvoyance revealed to me when I was still an adolescent— 'powers' that I naïvely (and quite unthinkingly) tried to exploit for personal ends. I did my best to point out, to those who really wanted to understand, the forest of symbols surrounding us—in the sacred books, in our physical characteristics (those signposts of our past incarnations) and even in fashion, since that is still my chosen artistic field. All signs that, like a footbridge thrown over the void, sometimes allow us to enter a world that is not 'other' (it is always ours), but a world composed of 'meaning' and 'light', in which life's chaos will be no more than a dream. In reality, as a famous scientist has reminded us, chance is only what we cannot yet explain.

This conviction was strikingly brought home to me by an extraordinary vision which I have already described elsewhere, although I dared not tell of all I had seen. What I experienced was an astral voyage, an experience of the kind that has been shared by a number of others.

Readers of my previous book may remember that at the age of seven, when I was lying on my bed half-asleep and trying to obliterate time, my spirit rose slowly from my inert body and I was suddenly transported into the presence of a strong light whose source I could not make out. I gradually realised that I was reliving the moment before my 'descent' to earth, my last incarnation . . .

*   *   *

I was no longer conscious of my own existence, for I was fused with the source of all light and all knowledge. I was face to face with the Divinity, that vast centre which vibrates to the rhythm of the cosmos. Instinctively I knew that I was on the Seventh Vibratory Plane, the highest plane, where everything is simply Essence. I no longer had bodily shape, I was a simple entity, vibratory and luminous. For me every second that passed seemed like eternity. I was full of joy, contemplating the immensity and communicating with the infinite. Joy because I was no longer myself, being Him. Overcome, because I was at one with the Totality.

But this ecstasy was rudely interrupted. Another kind of presence disturbed my joy. Turning away from the One, I made out what looked to me like large Xs of light which, by a sort of natural anthropomorphism, I came to call the 'Elders', because they seemed to me to be as old as the world, in the most literal sense.

These Elders, twenty-four of them, observed me gravely. I asked them an unspoken question, for we communicated without uttering a word:

'What do you want of me?'

'You must go down again, be re-embodied.'

My response was immediate. 'No!' I shouted. 'I have completed my *karma* on planet Earth . . .'

'Look!' was their answer.

The globe of our Blue Planet appeared to me. A being was approaching it. This entity, which I guessed to be none other than myself, was going to choose a human body in which to incarnate itself. And that was where I saw the destiny of mankind.

I found myself projected into an absolutely terrifying adult world. Then the horrifying scenes I was to witness throughout my terrestrial existence unfolded before my terror-stricken eyes.

First of all came the war which set Spain, my native land, ablaze and the first bombing raids with a civilian population as their target, on the little town of Guernica. This fratricidal strife was to scar my youthful years deeply, because my father was shot by the supporters of Franco and I had to flee with my mother over the snowclad mountains to France, which then became the land where I found refuge.

Next I saw the horrors of the 1939—45 war, with its bloodthirsty dictators, its barbarous regimes and its death-camps. I heard the screams of the women and children sacrificed and gassed at Auschwitz, Buchenwald and elsewhere. To my misfortune and that of humanity, history has subsequently confirmed my visions.

Then I saw crime gradually conquer the whole planet. I saw the world, originally so luminous, grow darker and darker. I saw it plunge inexorably into oppression, misery and destruction.

The unbearable spectacle did not stop there. For I also saw World War III, or the ultimate abomination. It was no longer a confrontation between nation and nation, but a chaotic conflict. The fighting raged from street to street, from window to window, the sole aim being the joy of killing someone else regardless of who they were . . . The discord spread like the plague from village to village, from province to province, until it covered the whole surface of the planet. Religious war, ethnic war, war for survival, total war . . .

Then the Blue Planet was plunged into terrible darkness from which all that emerged were screams of terror and panic. The three days of Jehovah, foretold by the prophets, had arrived . . .

At the end of the three days, I saw the survivors roaming like beasts, then tearing each other to pieces to indulge in cannibalism and other unspeakable crimes.

All of a sudden I saw the obscene Beast rise up . . .

And everything ceased.

Then I felt myself being drawn down towards the Earth, carried away in a flash, pierced by a terrible pain, the price I must pay for my passage from the state of ethereal light to the state of matter. A sharp point had just nailed me to the heart of the embodiment. Now I was reincarnated. I had chosen a couple who would turn out to be my parents. So began a new existence in the form of Francisco Rabaneda-Cuervo, who was later to adopt the name of Paco Rabanne.

* * *

It was a long time before I could bring myself to tell anyone about this extraordinary revelation which had left me panting on my bed, unable to move. My few attempts to confide foundered on my elder brother's mockery or my mother's amused incredulity. My astral voyage gradually became nothing more than a childish dream. Or maybe a nightmare . . . At all events, I stuffed my dream in my pocket and my handkerchief on top of it.

Or rather I made an unconscious effort to retain only its most positive elements, I mean the discovery of an immaterial world, 'magical' in the higher sense of the word, that coexisted with and enriched our own. There was a close correlation between these two universes, these two different vibratory planes. One was a tracing of the other, so that the world now looked like a hologram to me. In other words, my body in its infinite smallness was in the image of the cosmos in its infinite greatness. On the other hand, my being was not confined to its existing body nor to its actual existence. It had been incarnated many times, in different epochs, not just to satisfy some idle yearning for material pleasures, but rather to become refined, to lighten its *karma*—in fact gradually to rid itself of faults accumulated in the past.

In this way, you see, I retained everything that gave a meaning to life, especially the certainty of oneness of being with a world that no longer frightened me. If I was a part of the All, what had I to fear from it? At the same time I kept silent about the most distressing parts of my vision. A child of seven had no need of those apocalyptic scenes. Or rather, he preferred to push them back into the innermost depths of his being.

Unfortunately, historical events have confirmed the first series of dreadful images impressed on my mind. Yet I have said and I repeat it in terror: the worst is yet to come . . .

*

It may surprise you that anyone holding such convictions should have continued to pursue a career as a couturier, but I did so, with high ambitions. Wouldn't it have made more sense to seek refuge in a cave in the Atlas mountains? Or again, why haven't I used all my resources to build some kind of atomic bomb shelter in which I could one day escape the horrors that everything predicts for us?

The fact is that, far from condemning me to renunciation or inactivity, these apocalyptic visions undoubtedly encouraged me to lead my material and spiritual life to the best of my abilities. I shall have the opportunity to explain myself later on; for the moment, all I need say is that they have paradoxically given me hope and above all a strong will which have never failed me since.

For a long time my family lived the modest and often reclusive life of a family of anti-Franco refugees in a France which was soon to find itself under German occupation. I was a curious child and a lover of nature, becoming ever more conscious of the links that united me with it. I was as enthusiastic about the biological sciences as I was about the 'magic' which drove me to delve more deeply into an intimate knowledge of our world.

Later, I went to Paris to join the School of Architecture at the Beaux-Arts. These were my student years during which I specialised in the history of art and ancient civilisations with a passion that was all the greater because I found in them a disturbing echo of my former lives. My reading led me increasingly towards secret doctrines and the decipherment of sacred and prophetic messages.

Little by little I abandoned architecture to devote myself to fashion. Admittedly it was a bold step from architectural drawings to sketches, from model buildings to making up various kinds of accessories, but I had no hesitation in taking it. Until the day when, in a somewhat provocative mood, I presented my first fashion collection, for which I had Amazons encased in chain-mail parading before an audience that was half highly enthusiastic and half absolutely scandalised. In the process I caused one of the biggest uproars in the history of *haute couture*. My career as a designer was launched . . .

At the same time, still haunted by my childhood visions and disturbed by the regular appearance of a 'supra' sensibility which I dared not yet identify with mediumistic powers, I continued my spiritual quest, seeking in sacred and learned books confirmation of a truth I already felt in my bones.

I also found this confirmation—and still find it today—in practising meditation which reminds me of my link with the beyond and that I belong to a long chain anchored in the night of the world.

*

For some time now, however, my meditations have been proving increasingly traumatic. Suppressed for years, the horrific images inflicted on me as a warning by the Twenty-Four Elders are recurring today with greater force than ever. I see nothing but massacres and desolation everywhere.

One word in particular echoes in my mind, a word that bursts on my ears, trumpeted unceasingly by my spiritual guides: 'Emergency! Emergency!'

It is this alarm call that impels me to speak out again today. If there is an emergency, it is because the mounting dangers are growing faster and faster as the end of our millennium approaches. No one disagrees with me about this. One would have to be deaf and blind to ignore the perils looming on the horizon. And if we are still not fully aware of them, it is perhaps precisely because we are already at the heart of this period of disturbances and confusion that heralds the great cataclysm. An actor finds it difficult to judge the whole play, just as an infantryman has only a very limited view of the battlefield.

But from now on it is no longer a question of learning how to decipher the hidden signs, all we have to do is open our eyes. Racial conflicts, famine or even the destruction of our planet by pollution are no longer mirages we see vaguely on the horizon and may have our doubts about—these dangers make up our reality right now!

'Emergency!' if we are to have any chance of changing a course that could drag us towards the ultimate catastrophe.

'Emergency!' for we are coming to the end of Time. I say the end of Time advisedly, because I mean the end of our present Time, not the end of the World. For I must begin by clearing up a common misunderstanding. We are not talking about the end of all Time, a phrase often paraded hysterically by unscrupulous preachers to terrify their faithful flocks. Let's stop worrying! The end of the world which disaster movies and birds of ill omen thrive on is not coming tomorrow. The world is well, thank you very much. But the Earth indeed is ill. And its illness presages that we are on the verge of an important turning-point which could easily come about in the worst possible manner unless we are on our guard . . .

*   *   *

I know that people will accuse me of awakening (somewhat prematurely) a great dread of the year 2000, of the kind that prevailed, we are told, just before the year 1000.

This might well seem to be an especially opportune moment. We know what secret anxiety, what genuine anguish, the idea of the change of a millennium can arouse in us. Relayed to us by the phantasmagoria of science-fiction, our unconscious portrays this notorious threshold of the year 2000 as the most perilous of capes to be rounded, or as a reef on which we are bound to break up. In fact we are dealing here with a phenomenon whose sole basis is entirely psychological.

The best proof of this is undoubtedly that this milestone date is a pure convention. The number in itself means little or nothing and this sudden upheaval we are so afraid of has no real existence, except on our calendars.

The continuing debates regarding the exact dating of the Christian era are well known. Indeed, I remember my surprise when, as a young reader, I discovered that King Herod the Great (who, Matthew tells us, had all the children in Bethlehem massacred in the hope of destroying the future 'King of the Jews', who had just been born), that this bloodthirsty Herod died four years before the 'official' birth of Jesus Christ, according to all the biblical scholars and encyclopaedists!

Bothered by this kind of muddled chronology, I learnt that the decision to count the years from the birth of Christ went back to AD 532 and that the idea came from Denys the Small. The first day of the Roman year 754 became 1 January of year 1 of the Christian era.

It emerged later, however, that Denys the Small had made a mistake and that Christ was born at least four years before the date chosen. In spite of this, it was agreed to continue to follow this Dionysian calendar. But any one of you can verify in his encyclopaedia that Jesus Christ was born several years (between four and seven, depending on the interpretation) before Jesus Christ!

In other words, as I write we should not be in 1993, but in 1997, or even in the year 2000! So this famous 'year 2000' we await with such dread should really be the year 2004, or even 2007!

Here we have an example of fuzzy dating that should put us on our guard against any whiff of panic and encourage us to mistrust even more those who brandish the exact date of the end of our millennium like some bogey.

*

The other excellent reason for not scrutinising our calendar too minutely is that it would be a monstrous self-delusion to believe that a planetary upheaval should occur on a date which is only a milestone for us Christians and Westerners. In point of fact, our year 2000 will not mark the end of a millennium for the Arabs or the Jews. For the former we shall be in the year 1421 of the Hegira and for the Jews in the year 5760. So let us be on our guard against fixation on a date which is only 'fateful' for a fraction of mankind, even if it is our own.

Moreover, most historians specialising in the Middle Ages agree that the celebrated wave of panic in the year 1000 was a twofold piece of fantasy. Firstly, because this transition from three to four figures was not followed by any spectacular catastrophe. Secondly, and most importantly, because it seems that this wave of panic did not actually take place. A few local preachers are known to have announced the coming of the Apocalypse, but their words raised only a feeble echo, mainly because the means of communication at the time were very limited. The panic of the year 1000 seems to have been an invention by later centuries.

So let us forget the date of the year 2000 as far too precise and conventional to have any kind of meaning for or influence on our common destiny.

*   *   *

Then why should we worry? you will say. Why should the transition from the second to the third millennium not take place as peacefully as the passage from the first to the second?

There is little doubt why. Factors more relevant than our official system of dating are involved here. Everything indicates that mankind is now at the end of a *cycle*, a concept that has far more to say about our destiny than the millennium.

It is easy to see that our whole life is made up of cycles, in the image of the cosmos itself. That should not surprise us, for 'that which is below is like that which is above and vice versa', according to the golden rule laid down by Hermes Trismegistus, author of the *Corpus Hermeticum*, an inexhaustible source of inspiration for Greek and Christian thinkers. Thus night drives day away until dawn, just as sleep drives out the fatigues acquired the day before. The seasons die and are reborn, and with them most of the flora and fauna. Above our heads, the celestial ballet is renewed with a watchmaker's precision, each star resuming its place in this heavenly choreography at regular intervals. Everyone knows that what we call a year corresponds to the time taken by the Earth to make a complete revolution round the Sun, in other words 365¼ days.

But we are less familiar with what is known as the 'precessional year', even though it controls the fate of humanity over very much greater periods. Those readers who are experts in astronomy must forgive me for the simplified explanation that follows. At this point it is enough for us to understand the principle of this cycle, without going into detail.

While revolving round the Sun, the Earth also rotates on its own axis. But this movement is disturbed in a complicated way by the asymmetry of our planet and by solar and lunar attraction. As a result the Earth is affected by another movement, which we call precession. It consists of a very slow rotation, like that of a spinning top, around its orbital plane, known as the ecliptic. Thus the Earth's axis is not fixed in relation to the stars and the celestial vault.

It shifts by one degree every 72 years (the length of a human life) and makes a complete cycle in 25,920 years. The present Pole Star is only valid for our epoch; in a few thousand years another will have taken its place.

25,920 years. Twenty-six millennia . . . That is the duration of the precessional year. It sounds colossal to us, but it is only a brief spark compared with the history of the cosmos. The precessional year forms what the Greeks called the Great Year, at the end of which the Earth regains its exact place on the ecliptic.

Because it changes position slowly in relation to the sphere of the stars, the Earth's axis points, with the passage of time, from one constellation to another. So the Great Year is divided into 12 'months' of about 2,160 years each, to which all the signs of the stellar zodiac, Cancer, Gemini, Libra, and so on, correspond.

The last three signs were Taurus, Aries and Pisces. These signs have had strange echoes in the history of mankind, each one symbolising a new religion, or at least a new way of looking at the world.

Taurus was the favourite god of the ancient civilisations, especially the Indo-Mediterranean ones. The Vedic gods Indra and Shiva were associated with the bull, as were Osiris and Apis by the Egyptians. He may also take the name of El or Enlil among the Babylonians, but the bull always represents creative force and fecundity, the principal of life which sometimes exacts sacrifices, on the model of the famous Cretan Minotaur.

As for Aries, he covers the whole of the Hebraic period. We find his image everywhere in the Old Testament. When Moses destroyed the Golden Calf, he was first and foremost attacking the symbol of a former religion. It was the cult of El he was proscribing. It was a question of chaining the Minotaur, that is to say of taming man's appetites and resisting the intoxication of Dionysiac enchantments. The ram preserves the bull's ardour, but combines it with generosity and the ideal of justice.

Some two thousand years later, the era of Pisces began with the birth of Christ. Although the latter is often identified with the lamb, this is to signify his filial relationship with the Ram, but we know that the fish was the ideogram used as a 'password' by the early, persecuted Christians. Did not Jesus enter Jerusalem by the Gate of Fishes? From the miraculous catch of fish to the multiplication of the fishes, this symbolism is everywhere in the New Testament. Moreover, the Greek word *Ichthys*, meaning fish, corresponds to the initials of *Iesus Khristos Theou Uios Sôter*, translated as 'Jesus Christ, Son of God, Saviour'.

According to the astronomers, our entry into the constellation of Pisces dates to about 150 BC. Basing ourselves on an average duration of 2,160 years, passage into the age of Aquarius (the next sign 'pointed at' by the Earth's axis) should take place around 2010. After two millennia of the Christian era, we are going to experience a new moral and religious transformation . . .

No need for me to point out that such a spiritual change does not take place overnight. You are not going to wake up one fine day to find a new world and a different religion on your doorstep. Sometimes the passage takes centuries, symbols live on from one cycle to another, customs change gradually before falling into disuse and disappearing. We have been in a period of transition for some time now. The various troubles disturbing our planet and the moral crisis we are undergoing are the signs of this evolution. An evolution unlikely to take place peacefully . . .

*　　*　　*

The passage from one era to another, from one precessional 'month' to another, does not in itself constitute a planetary hazard. We shall see that it may even
be a chance for humanity, provided that humanity
accepts this movement instead of keeping it in check
and persisting in the path of error and apostasy.

If I believe that there is a genuine threat today, it
is because this zodiacal conversion is coupled with
an even more dramatic caesura, a veritable cyclical
revolution which confirms all the ancient traditions
with striking unanimity.

All these traditions divide the great history of mankind into four 'ages' of varying length, although they
are mathematically determined by the precessional
year. As they succeed each other they describe a slow
descent from light into darkness.

The first of these ages, which the Greeks call the
Golden Age and the Hindus the Krita Yuga, is the
longest because it lasts for a whole Great Year, that
is some 25,920 years. A glorious age of communion
with the Divine, it lasts for us Christians from the
Creation of Adam to the Fall and preoccupation with
the flesh.

The second age is the Silver Age or Treta Yuga to
the Hindus. It corresponds to three-quarters of a
Great Year, some 19,440 years, and already exhibits
a certain decadence, a passage from divine love to
duty. It is followed by the Bronze Age or Dwapara
Yuga, which lasts for half a precessional year and
comes under the sign of the passions. By and large
these two cycles cover our pre- and proto-history.

The Bronze Age takes us to the gates of antiquity,
to the birth of the Iron Age that regroups the three
precessional 'months' I have just mentioned, coming
under the signs of Taurus, Aries and Pisces. This
cycle of 6,480 years is the celebrated Kali Yuga of the
Hindus.

All the traditions describe the last-named cycle as

an age of increasing violence and darkness. For Hermes Trismegistus (*Corpus Hermeticum*) it is a period when:

> . . . no one will raise their eyes to heaven again; the pious man will be regarded as mad, the impious as wise . . . The soul and all its associated beliefs, according to which the soul is immortal by nature, will simply be laughed at . . . The Gods will separate themselves from men: a separation to be deplored!

For the Greeks, and for Hesiod in his *Works and Days*, during the Iron Age,

> the guest will no longer be dear to his host, nor friend to friend, nor brother to brother. Children will show nothing but contempt for their parents as soon as they grow old. They will refuse food to the old people who nourished them. No worth will be attached to the solemn oath, to the just or the good. Force will be the only right. Jealousy will cling to the steps of all humans, wretched suffering will be the lot of mortals: there will be no recourse against Evil.

Today we find ourselves at the very end of Kali Yuga, which the *Linga Purana*, a Hindu religious epic compiled around the fifth century BC, describes as follows:

> Indifference, sickness, hunger and fear will spread abroad. Serious droughts will be seen. The different regions of the world will join in conflict with each other. The sacred texts will no longer be respected. Men will be without morals, irritable and sectarian. False doctrines and deceitful writings will spread.

The number of princes and farmers will progressively decline. Most of the new chiefs will rise from among working men.

Foetuses will be killed inside their mothers' wombs. Thieves will become kings, kings will become thieves. Numerous will be the women who have relations with several men.

The earth shall produce abundantly in certain places and too little in others. The leaders will confiscate properties and put them to bad use.

There will be many displaced persons wandering from one country to another.

Upright men will give up playing an active part.

Ready-cooked food will be put on sale. The sacred books will be sold at every street corner. Young women will sell their virginity. The god of the clouds will be fickle in distributing the rains. There will be many beggars and unemployed. It will be impossible to trust anybody.

Degradation of the virtues and censure of hypocritical puritans will characterise the period at the end of Kali Yuga. Groups of bandits will organise themselves in town and country. Water will be scarce and fruit will be in short supply.

Many individuals will be perfidious, lewd and vile. They will wear their hair in disorder. Adventurers will assume the guise of monks, with shaven heads and orange-coloured vestments.

People afflicted with hunger and fear will take refuge in underground shelters.

Unqualified people will pass for experts in moral and religious matters.

Can't you recognise an accurate (and distressing) description of our contemporary world running through all these quotations? The Hindu text goes on to predict a terrible war that will reduce men to poor, starving, sick and desperate creatures. 'That is when some of them will begin to reflect.'

*   *   *

The rapid approach of the third millennium is not the only reason why I have felt the desire, even a pressing need, to ring the alarm bell at this particular moment. Based on the great sidereal revolutions, the ancient 'cyclologies' tell us that the world has reached a crucial turning-point.

My personal view of the world and human evolution points in the same direction. You will remember that during my astral voyage the Twenty-Four Elders had made me realise that I was on the Seventh Vibratory Plane, the plane of fusion with the All. All my subsequent meditations have convinced me that the history of man and his incarnations was laid out in a hierarchy of successive planes, according to the remoteness or closeness of his relations with the divine. Thus, the first plane is that of the lemurs and humanoids who have only just emerged from the animal kingdom. The second plane is that of cave-dwelling man distinguished by his upright carriage and the use of fire and tools. The third forms our actual state, that of incarnate man, hampered by his fleshly covering, but aspiring to the divine. Today the whole of creation yearns to rise to the Fourth Vibratory Plane, which will be distinguished by a preponderance of spirituality. To use a different terminology, we are witnessing the last days of *Homo sapiens*. Then will come the long-awaited reign of *Homo spiritualis*. Provided that *Homo destructor* does not intervene and prevent it!

Accession to a higher Vibratory Plane, arrival of *Homo spiritualis* or cyclical return to a new Golden Age . . . Once the miseries of the Apocalypse are over, man's long-term future promises to be a brilliant one . . . May I remind you that apocalypse does *not* mean destruction, as the generally accepted use of the word would have us believe, but Revelation. It is the disclosure of the divine message and the far-off destiny reserved for mankind.

*

But we shall have to undergo terrible ordeals to become worthy of receiving these secrets. This civilisation of ours, which has turned away from the face of God to become no more than a cold, impersonal system, must perish. The Book of Revelation tells us that many plagues, ranging from war to famine, must strike mankind before the New Jerusalem finally appears . . .

Can we escape these calamities, even though all the prophecies predict them? All the sacred books speak of the Day of Divine Wrath, when the sky will draw back like a scroll that is rolled up, when the Eternal shall cause mourning and solitude on earth . . . I am of course speaking of St John's apocalyptic prophecy, but also of those by Ezekiel, Isaiah and Daniel, or again the Books of Enoch and Jubilees, and Baruch's Syriac Apocalypse.

Side by side with these religious works, we find all the prophecies that we call 'private'—I mean those emanating from seers, soothsayers and other 'inspired' beings who have seen visions foretelling our future. I am thinking of Nostradamus, St Caesarius, St Malachy, Giovanni di Vatiguerro and others. There are also the Marian prophecies and anonymous texts such as the important prophecies of Prémol and Orval. There is no lack of material for those who want to calculate the exact date of our destiny. Like many before them, they will be forced to admit that the unanimity of all these texts lends them a disturbing weight.

*   *   *

Critics will object that these prophetic texts must not be taken at their face value. The main reason for this distrust, I am told, is that many of these predictions never come true. For example, we know that many preachers, relying on the Number of the Beast given in the Revelation of St John as 666, foretold the end of the world for 1666. Admittedly, the Londoners who were the victims of a vast conflagration in that year must have thought their last days had come, but one can hardly class that dramatic event as one of apocalyptic dimensions. I could quote many other examples of this nature. Among them was William Miller, founder of the Adventist Church, who ostentatiously proclaimed the Last Judgement for May 1843. As nothing happened, he trumpeted forth the date of March 1844, then October. Still nothing. Strangely enough, these missed appointments in no way discouraged Miller's adherents . . .

Many frauds have also been unmasked. They are what I would call hindsight prophecies. Working in 1830, say, it is easy enough to produce a prophecy reputedly dating to the sixteenth century discovered in the library of some monastery and foretelling Napoleon's epic career with great accuracy (and with good reason). The history of prophecy is signposted with such mystifications.

Some seers were the unwitting victims of fraud. For example, a few apocryphal quatrains were apparently added later to the famous *Centuries* by Nostradamus. Like this one, which obviously referred to Napoleon I:

In time to come the cocks shall drive out
the eagle from Arcole and Lodi in the
Italic land. Teutons, Hungarians,
Lombards, the Germanic army shall pack their
bags before the conquering Gauls.

It is easy to 'prognosticate' an event after it has happened. However, these vulgar manipulations should not tarnish the brilliance and authenticity of Nostradamus's predictions. In the first edition of his book in 1555, the soothsayer wrote (First Century, quatrain 35):

> The young lion shall overcome the old one
> on a martial field, in single combat,
> he will put out his eyes in their cage of gold,
> one of two kinds, then his foe will die an
>   agonising death.

A few years later, on 1 July 1559, King Henri II of France confronted the young Count Montgomery in a tournament. For the occasion he wore a blazon representing a lion. His adversary's lace broke and a long splinter of wood pierced the royal helmet. His eye put out, his skull pierced right through, Henri II died after several days of atrocious suffering.

*

Personally I think we must separate the wheat from the chaff. The Bible itself warns us to be very cautious of the self-proclaimed prophets who were not inspired by God. At the same time, we must be careful not to reject out of hand such predictions of the future. Just because a few impostors have insinuated themselves into the ranks of the prophets, we must not refuse to listen to words that are intended for us. 'They did not hearken,' says the Bible, 'they flouted the messengers of God, scorned their words and mocked their prophecies.' When people are sceptical of everything, they end up believing in nothing, and incredulity becomes unpardonable blindness.

We know, for example, that when Naziism was on the increase in Germany, many Jews were unwilling to believe that their lives were in danger, in spite of all the warnings. Perhaps they should have paid more attention to the Book of Jeremiah which, it is true, was also a promise of hope:

> The people of Israel shall be punished like no other people . . . After the slaughter and the scattering . . . I will bring them from the north country and gather them from the coasts of the earth . . . I will cause them to walk by the rivers of waters in a straight way. Hear the words of the Lord, O ye nations and declare it in the isles afar off and say, He that scattered Israel will gather him.

Could there be a clearer prediction of the death camps, the rebirth of the State of Israel and the massive return of the Jews to the Holy Land?

So disbelief in the prophecies would imply repudiating an important part of the Bible and the message of the Divinity, for the great prophets are indeed His spokesmen.

*

And why shouldn't 'private' predictions, too, carry a measure of truth? The great seers are not trying to convince, they are simply passing on orally a certainty that has been imposed on them from above. And whether or not we are prepared to accept their premonitions as 'inspired', honesty forces us to admit that they have often proved accurate, even if we do not understand the 'mechanism' that produced them.

We are quite prepared to admit that a person can 'sense' the death of another, even though they are thousands of miles apart. This is one of the phenomena of thought transmission to which science is devoting considerable attention today. History has many stories to tell us on the subject. Here is an example. In the year 96 at Ephesus, the philosopher Apollonius of Tyana was addressing a small group of followers when he suddenly broke off, apparently dumbfounded. Then he struck the ground several times with his stick before saying to his audience:

'Rejoice, for the tyrant is dead!'

At first they did not understand him. They thought he was crazy. But later they learnt that at the very same moment in Rome, a freedman called Stephanus had struck the cruel tyrant Domitian a mortal blow.

If premonitions can conquer space in this way, why could they not conquer time, too? The phenomenon is rare, but it has been authenticated. Certain seers, gifted with paranormal powers, are subject to 'visions' which suddenly tell them about the past of someone they did not know—and met quite by chance. Then they are capable of recounting the most outstanding events in this person's past. Or of predicting events that will affect his future.

Readers may know the following anecdote involving Nostradamus. One day, while travelling in Italy, he met a group of humble young Franciscan friars. Suddenly, moved by an impulse that he himself could not explain, he knelt on the ground before one of the friars and began to kiss his vestment. His companions, taken aback by this mystifying gesture, burst out laughing.

'What are you up to?' they asked Nostradamus.

'I must submit and kneel to His Holiness,' replied the famous soothsayer.

Many years later, the Franciscans must surely have remembered the scene. The young friar before whom Nostradamus had knelt was none other than Felice Peretti, who became Cardinal of Montalte and later, in 1585, Pope, under the name of Sixtus V.

Other clairvoyants seem to be able to 'foresee' the

fate of a group of people. No one at Cincinnati airport will have forgotten the repeated telephone calls made in May 1979 by a certain David Booth, who declared:

'For several days I have been dreaming about an aviation disaster that is going to happen very soon.'

Officials took no notice of him, laughing heartily at what they thought were the nightmares of a lunatic. But the day after his last call, American Airlines Flight 191 crashed shortly after take-off. There were no survivors.

Science-fiction also provides examples of fascinating premonitions. After the wreck of the *Titanic* in 1912, people remembered a book that had gone unnoticed when it was published in 1898. Written by Morgan Robertson, *The Wreck of the Titan* was the story of a giant liner which struck an iceberg and sank while making its first crossing of the Atlantic! The coincidences with reality were extraordinary: the *Titan* and the *Titanic* had the same tonnage, the same cruising speed, even the same number of propellers and passengers. The month of the shipwreck and the name of the captain also tallied exactly! What can one say about that?

I might also mention that many details in Jules Verne's book *From the Earth to the Moon*, written in 1865, coincide with the story of the actual conquest of space achieved a century later. The emplacement of the launching pad in Florida, the number of astronauts, the landing in the Pacific—they are all there. Even the names of two of the astronauts show strange similarities: Ardans and Nicholl in Jules Verne, Aldrin and Collins in reality.

It does not need a novelist, however, to imagine what will happen in the future. There was a well-known figure in England called Mother Shipton, a prophetess born in Yorkshire in 1488, of whom it was said that she had a hideous body and face, but an astounding intelligence and an amazing capacity for clairvoyance. What did this woman tell us at the end of the fifteenth century?

> Carriages without horses shall go
> and accidents fill the world with woe.
> Around the world thoughts shall fly
> in the twinkling of an eye.
> World upside down shall be
> and gold found at the root of a tree.
> Through hills men shall ride
> and no horse or ass be by their side.
> Under water men shall walk,
> shall ride, shall sleep, shall talk.
> In the air men shall be seen
> in white, in black and in green.
> Iron in the water shall float
> as easy as a wooden boat.
> Gold shall be found, and found
> in land that is not known.
> Iron and water shall more wonders do.
> All England's sons that plough the land
> shall be seen, books in hand.
> Learning shall so ebb and flow
> the poor shall most with them know.
> Water shall flow where corn shall grow;
> corn shall grow where waters flow.

Could anything be more obvious? We do not need some farfetched interpretation to see that these brief lines foretell the great discoveries of the nineteenth and twentieth centuries, from the automobile to telecommunications, not to mention submarines and nuclear power . . .

And what are we to make of the fifteenth-century inscription carved on a grave-stone in the cemetery at Kirby, also in England, which says that when images look alive and seem to move of themselves, when ships travel under the sea like fish, and men outdo the birds and climb the Heavens, half the World will be engulfed in blood.

*   *   *

I hope that my readers will not see this lengthy build-up as a way of sanctioning me, too, to put myself forward as a soothsayer. They need not worry, I have no such intention! I am simply an avid reader, as well as a witness of our time. I try to be constantly in touch with events happening here below and to find in them echoes of ancient warnings.

Where the news from the media presents the image of a fragmented world, where reporters take us from one country and one subject to another, I see signs that establish a coherent order. The increase of fanaticism, ethnic conflicts, the violence of urban life and the famine affecting many African countries do not look like isolated events to me. They are working out a plot that is growing ever clearer, a whole in which we are all involved. If catastrophe is close, the least we can do is to try to understand it. Surely clarity is the best guarantee of all positive action?

But the fact that I wish to bear witness here to the anxieties that now assail me (almost constantly) in no way implies that I want to set myself up as a prophet! I am only obeying the feeling of urgency that drives me, sometimes to the point of revolt. Surely I cannot be blamed for voicing my fears? If they turn out to be unfounded, no one will be happier than I. 'Woe unto you that desire the day of the Lord! . . . Shall not the day of the Lord be darkness, and not light?' Amos tells us in the Old Testament (5:18 and 20). It is my dearest wish to be proved wrong. But should the opposite be the case, I need not blame myself for keeping silent in the face of events.

Nor should anyone say that I am playing into the

hands of some sect or other. I beg those who read these lines to use their critical judgement at all times. Above all, I am against prejudices, those blinkers that prevent us from looking reality in the eye. When it comes to sects, I only belong to one— the trade union of *haute couture*, absolutely indispensable to me!

*

Some of you will smile when you read what follows; you will doubt everything I say and refuse to join in this Cassandra-like game.

Or you will point out that the prophecies I mention make skilful use of ambiguity. The story of Croesus, who was planning to make war on the Persians, is often quoted in this connection. In order to weigh up his chances of success, he consulted the Delphic oracle, which gave him this answer: 'A great empire will be destroyed.' Sure of his victory, Croesus gave battle. He suffered a heavy defeat and was actually captured. An empire had indeed been destroyed, but it was not the one he had in mind.

Many prophets express themselves like this, in ambiguous and picturesque language that one must know how to decipher without getting lost in the forest of symbols. But there is really no room for misunderstanding in the interpretations that can be made today. This 'empire', this world, whose destruction is foretold, is *ours*, it is the planet Earth.

Lastly, some of you may remind me that there has always been someone in every epoch to declare that a moment of crisis was at hand and that the world had only a few more years of life. The overimaginative interpreters of prophecies have constantly had to amend their predictions and put the fatal date forward.

Today, however, there is a difference of scale. Indeed, for the first time in the history of mankind, the prophetic warnings and signs predicting the Apocalypse no longer look like the vulgar inventions of science fiction or cranks: they are part of our everyday reality.

And in the forefront of those who are rushing to sound the alarm are not a few lunatics with deranged minds, but our most eminent scientists.

Chapter 2

WHEN SCIENTISTS AND INITIATES MEET

A time will come when men will no longer look at the world as an object worthy of their admiration and their reverence.

Hermes Trismegistus

'We have only one or two decades left in which to fight against our current threats and the prospect of an enormously diminished humanity.'

What fanatical visionary could have hurled such an alarmist prophecy in the face of the world? What bird of ill omen dared to predict such an early deadline for disaster?

Unfortunately for our peace of mind, this sentence did not come from the mouth of some embittered, publicity-seeking preacher. It is an extract from the *Washington Appeal*, a text drafted and signed quite recently, in 1992, by 1,500 scholars of international repute, among them some hundred Nobel Prizewinners.

Obviously we are not dealing with a gathering of crackpots. Ever at the bedside of our ailing Earth, these people know its state of health inside out. It is hard for unbelievers and complacent optimists to reject as unfounded fears based on a statistical and empirical report on the present situation.

Nevertheless, honesty obliges me to add that not all the scientists have ratified the conclusions of the *Washington Appeal*. Some of them have magnanimously granted us a respite of fifty, or even a hundred years . . .

But they are all extremely pessimistic about our chances of survival, given the frantic speed at which our planet is being exploited. In spite of all their warnings, scientists are finding it quite hard to shake people out of their general indifference. If mankind and its rulers do not realise (and fast) the urgency of the situation, scientists say that they can no longer take *any responsibility*. Some of them are afraid that we have already reached the point of no return.

For the threats menacing our Blue Planet are so numerous that we no longer know which we should tackle first, even though many, if not all of them, have been predicted for centuries, even millennia! But we have turned deaf ears to the warnings, we have chosen not to use our eyes. And the most worrying feature to me is that, fully informed though we are, we are still doing nothing, or next to nothing, to try to avert the terrible fate we are preparing for ourselves. Will it be too late to check the frightening speed at which dangers are accumulating?

Everywhere I look, I see that we are into 'reduced time', the time during which everything happens much faster. Is it mere chance that the year 1991 experienced a quite unprecedented number of catastrophes? This information comes, not from me, but from the Insurance Institute's centre for documentation and information. It enumerates more than 100 floods, hurricanes, volcanic eruptions and earthquakes. On top of that there were 50 major fires, the same number of serious collisions, 44 shipwrecks and 28 air disasters. Never before has the world had to pay such a high ecological and human tribute. And 1992 has been no kinder—far from it.

Yet in my opinion these are still merely 'warnings', however deadly they may be. What specialists in the biosphere would have us believe is far more alarming. Ironically enough, they are only expressing in

statistical terms what the prophets have been clam-
ouring for centuries and centuries.

Let us recall the terrible words of St John, speaking of the Apocalypse that lies ahead: 'Thy wrath is
come, and the time of the dead that they should be
judged . . . and (thou) shouldest destroy them which
destroy the earth . . .'

*   *   *

The first threat I want to mention here would be
the most unfounded if a recent discovery had not
suddenly brought it within the bounds of possibility.
In 1989, three French astronomers using the telescope at the observatory on the Côte d'Azur spotted
a large asteroid approaching the Earth! They named
this astral object Toutatis, doubtless as a reminder
of the terror felt of old by our ancestors the Gauls,
of whom it was said that they were afraid of nothing,
except that the sky might fall on their heads.

Will this terror prove to be justified? Impossible,
you will say . . . And yet such a phenomenon would
not be without precedent. We have already had one
narrow escape—in March 1989, when a medium-
sized asteroid (about 300 metres in diameter)
dubbed 1989 FC passed by our planet at a distance of
some 700,000 kilometres, that is twice the distance
from the Earth to the Moon. Nothing to get excited
about, you will say. True, the distance seems more
than reasonable: at all events, it was enough to spare
us from any unpleasant repercussions. But on a cosmic scale you could say that the 'bullet' had come
close. If it had collided with the Earth, 1989 FC could
have formed a crater 500 metres deep and 15 kilometres in diameter, and created a shock wave capable of wiping out all traces of life over an area
equivalent to the Ile-de-France.

*

Our solar system is teeming with such asteroids and other comets. It is currently estimated that a hundred of them of various sizes are describing an orbit intersecting the Earth's. And as astronomy progresses, new ones are constantly being discovered. Fortunately for us, our planet is equipped with an effective means of protection. Meteorites approaching too close are checked and finally reduced to fragments by the dense layers of our atmosphere. Then they fall to earth in the form of particles or harmless pebbles.

But this protection is not always enough, as has already been demonstrated. And we do not have to go back all that far to find it. In 1908 a meteorite fell near Tunguska in Siberia (luckily it was not a very large one). Passengers on the Trans-Siberian Express saw a great ball of fire shoot across the sky. In its wake it left the taïga devastated for dozens of kilometres, snapping trees like matches. The meteorite disintegrated before making contact with the earth, but the explosion made the ground quake, while a gale-force wind tore down the huts of the Tunguse tribe, breaking doors and windows for 60 kilometres around. The inhabitants thought that an old Siberian myth had come true, in which it was said that the Earth would be wiped out by a deluge of fire. By 'chance' this meteorite fell in a sparsely populated area. Imagine the catastrophe it would have caused if it had landed on a large city!

But we must remember that it was a small meteorite. Scientists have tried to estimate the damage that would be caused by a heavenly body with a mass of a thousand billion tons, equivalent (only) to a cube ten kilometres square. The energy released at the time of the collision would raise the temperature to 200° Celsius. The shock produced by the impact would cause titanic earthquakes. If the meteorite fell in the sea, it would do nothing to solve our housing problems. Enormous tidal waves would submerge the land beneath waters as high as the Eiffel Tower, sweeping everything before them. The tectonic plates of the earth's crust would clash, swallowing up the continents; faults would gape open and every volcano would become active, belching out floods of lava.

Admittedly, such a cataclysm is unlikely. According to the astronomers, the chances of it happening are very small indeed. Yet the fact remains that it could happen tomorrow. We can still find vestiges of vast craters caused by ancient meteors, wherever erosion has not completely obliterated them. One of these craters, in Mexico, is nearly 200 kilometres in diameter. Geologists calculate that it was formed some 65 million years ago, a date that causes some concern because it coincides with the disappearance of the dinosaurs. Any that did survive the actual cataclysm would have succumbed to the cooling of the earth that followed. For the shock would have caused enormous masses of rock to be pulverised in the stratosphere. The resultant dust would have spread and formed a thick layer in the sky, blocking out the sun's rays and reducing the temperature of our terrestrial globe. Many animal and vegetable species would have been wiped off the face of the earth. The age of the dinosaurs had come to an end. One cycle had ended, another came to life. This period corresponds with the transition from the Cretaceous to the Tertiary . . .

As you can see, it would only need a meteorite one kilometre in diameter to cause, not the final destruction of the Earth, but a catastrophe on a global scale. The collision would shoot into the sky an enormous geyser of tens of thousands of fragments of rock which would then fall back to earth at tremendous speed. This rain of fire could cause the death of billions of people, as well as the destruction of dwellings and the disappearance of vegetation and harvests. Was it not a phenomenon of this type that Nostradamus was referring to when he wrote in the Preface to his Prophecies: 'Fire mixed with stones shall fall in such quantities that no one could remain in one place if they did not wish to be struck down'?

And surely the fall of a meteorite is also foretold in the Revelation of St John (8:7): 'And as it were a great mountain burning with fire was cast into the sea: and the third part of the sea became blood.' And again (6: 12—13): 'There was a great earthquake; and the sun became black as sackcloth of hair, and the moon became as blood. And the stars of heaven fell onto the earth, even as a fig tree casteth her untimely figs when she is shaken of a mighty wind.'* If the Heavens wax wrath, it is not surprising that punishment comes from the sky . . .

*

Will the recently discovered asteroid Toutatis be the instrument of divine anger? As I write these lines, I hear that it has just passed us by at a distance equal to about ten times that which separates us from the Moon. Will it be coming our way again? Was this a missed rendezvous by way of warning? If it is not Toutatis, perhaps it might be his brother.

The Koran refers to a similar event: 'The heavens will melt and fall in pieces . . . Carried into the air, the earth and the mountains will be reduced to dust in a flash.' The cloud of dust caused by the impact of an asteroid and the awakening of volcanic activity in the four corners of the earth would probably block out the Sun for many days. Is that when we shall see

---

* The use of the past tense is normal in sacred prophecies. It does not mean that the events have already happened. It is rather that timeless visions like this, which are part of the overall plan of world history, are already written down.

the celebrated 'Three Days of the Lord', the three days of darkness about which the Bible tells us?

Of course we could imagine a different scenario leading to an identical result. The upheaval caused by a stellar body might displace the earth's axis. We read in Isaiah (24:19—20): 'The earth is utterly broken down, the earth is clean dissolved, the earth is moved exceedingly. The earth shall reel to and fro like a drunkard, and shall be removed like a cottage; and the transgression thereof shall be heavy upon it.'

Such a shift of axis could upset or temporarily halt the earth's rotation in relation to the sun. Then one half of the globe would be exposed to the sun's rays for several days, while the other half would be plunged into a total, glacial darkness. Once again the Three Days of the Lord . . .

Obviously these are only suppositions. There is no cause for alarm . . . so long as a meteorite does not come too close. It is not the intention of the sacred texts to terrify us, but to warn us and encourage us to be vigilant. But if the Cosmos so wills it, our path will once again cross that of Toutatis or some other asteroid, and the sky will fall on our heads.

Meanwhile, let us keep an eye on the stars. We have nothing to lose—quite the reverse—by concentrating our eyes and our souls on the firmament.

*   *   *

Unfortunately for us, the Earth is exposed to dangers that are much less hypothetical and far more pressing than the fall of a meteorite. The good news, however, is that we have more influence over them than we do over the orbit of an astral body . . .

All the scientists agree that overpopulation is threat number one. Nothing else can give us a better idea of the sudden, extraordinary speed-up of the dangers facing us. For the population explosion is a recent phenomenon, corresponding roughly to the age of Pisces, the age of increase. The total number of human beings stayed very low for millennia. It is estimated that world population at the time of Christ was of the order of 200,000,000 human beings. In 1750 it was still only 700,000,000. Then suddenly, at the end of Kali Yuga, there has been a spurt. Ironically enough, this population explosion is partly due to the benefits of science, which has finally managed to reduce infant mortality and prolong life expectation. So we grew from 1.1 billion in 1850 to 2.5 billion in the middle of the present century.

Then the population started galloping. In 1975 we passed the four billion mark, 12 years later that of five billion and today the latest estimates put forward the figure of 5.6 billion. Every day, I repeat *every day*, 220,000 babies are born! Two per second . . . Today the astronomical figure of ten billion inhabitants of the Earth is widely predicted for around 2050, although up to now it would have been only in the realms of pure fantasy.

When we realise that half the present population of the globe is living below the poverty line, is even constantly threatened with famine, we are entitled to ask what kind of fate will lie in store for the surplus five billion individuals. How can we meet their needs when so many people today have barely enough for survival? Worst of all, the poverty that now exists among a huge proportion of mankind is the only reaon why we ourselves survive. If the whole planet lived at the same rate as the rich countries, which are possessed by the demon of frenzied consumerism, we might as well throw in the towel now.

We should remember this sentence from the Sanskrit epic, the *Mahabharata* (Song 12, 248, 13–17) which has an ominous ring to it when we think of our own situation: 'The annihilation of the human race will occur when the Creator's only way of ending the disastrous and unforeseen multiplication of human beings will be the total destruction of the world.'

* * *

For while the population increase continues at a breakneck pace, our food production cannot keep pace with it. The gap between the number of mouths to feed and our resources is constantly widening. Today famine is not only causing terrible ravages in Somalia, it also threatens a large part of Africa, not to mention Asia and South America. Let us hearken to the early sixteenth-century soothsayer Giovanni di Vatiguerro, who drew a terrifying picture of the misfortunes to come at the end of the twentieth century in his *Liber Mirabilis (Book of Wonders)*: 'There will be an astonishing and cruel famine which will be so great and of such a kind throughout the universe, but especially in the western regions, that no one will have heard of its like since the beginning of the world.' A proclamation that was echoed by Nostradamus in Quatrain 67 of his First Century:

The great famine that I sense approaching,
often turning, then becoming universal,
so great and long that people will tear
the roots from the tree and the child from the
breast.

As these two clairvoyants warn us, the West, where plenty seems to reign, is not immune from famine. This could result from breaks in the food chain of the kind our assaults on the environment are gradually creating. Or from contamination of cultivable land after a nuclear war . . .

For a short while, in our blind faith in 'progress', we thought that the famous Green Revolution was going to solve all our problems. Thanks to science, we would be able to make spectacular increases in crop yields and so nurture all the Earth's children. Hybrid species were created that could be harvested up to three times a year. In this way it was hoped to maintain the balance between the population and food production. Unfortunately we know today that this was a Utopian dream. We seem to have been pursuing a cause that was lost from the very start. More seriously, the Green Revolution needlessly endangered the environment by the intensive use of pesticides and chemical fertilisers. There have been many prophecies telling us that one day the trees will no longer bear fruit and that arable land will be reduced to an unproductive film of soil.

*   *   *

The population explosion would not be a catastrophe in itself if it did not entail the destruction of our environment. Overpopulation brings in its train a whole procession of disasters. For we must be housed and fed . . . and we must consume. In the underdeveloped countries overpasturage leads to the spread of deserts, and every day, in the rich countries, tens of square kilometres of cultivable land are lost to encroaching concrete.

Prey to an insatiable appetite, we are using up more and more rapidly the resources that the Earth has put at our disposal. We spend without thinking, we throw natural energy such as coal and oil out of the window, we shamelessly exploit our mineral wealth. 'The Earth will be respected solely for its mineral treasures', says the *Vishnu Purana*, a Hindu text dating to many centuries BC.

Yet we, who thought these reserves inexhaustible, are amazed to find that the exhaustion of our oil reserves is now calculated in decades! At our current rate of consumption, in 50 years according to some, 80 according to others, there will not be a single drop

of oil left. And that is only one of several examples.
Our planet cannot be subjected to such plundering
indefinitely. A radical change in our behaviour and
our rate of consumption is therefore essential as a
basic condition of our survival.

*

Nevertheless, human thoughtlessness continues to
disfigure the Earth with terrible scars. Seen from the
air, our planet is unrecognisable today. Overpopulation (once again) stimulates a reckless acceleration
of the process of deforestation. Millions of hectares of
trees, those trees striving to rise towards the Fourth
Vibratory Plane with a rustle of silvery leaves, are
felled every year. Do you realise that, before the
arrival of the Europeans, North America could boast
of some 3.2 million square kilometres of forest?
Today there are no more than 0.2 million left.

As for the tropical rainforests, a sort of safety-belt
surrounding the globe, their regular felling goes on
at a frightening rate. The forests of the Ivory Coast
and Nigeria have practically disappeared. In fifty
years' time the same will be true of the whole planet!
Knowing as we do how much our very existence is
dependent on these vast forested areas, we may well
ask ourselves about the fate of mankind. Surely
humanity deserves to be punished for what some
have called 'the greatest biological crime ever perpetrated by man'? We should remember Isaiah's
curse (33:1): 'Woe to thee that spoilest, and thou
wast not spoiled; and dealest treacherously, and they
dealt not treacherously with thee! When thou shalt
cease to spoil, thou shalt be spoiled.' Entire civilisations are going to disappear, immense areas will be
transformed into scrubland or deserts by excessive
land clearance and agricultural overexploitation.
The trees will no longer be there to convert carbon
dioxide into oxygen. Without their action, the

atmosphere will be overloaded with carbon dioxide, which will intensify the greenhouse effect, causing the planet to heat up. Knowing that an increase of one degree in the globe's temperature would cause the flooding of countries such as Bangladesh, the Netherlands and the Polynesian atolls, we have good reason to tremble . . .

Deforestation also endangers other vital resources. Innumerable vegetable and animal species will be wiped out along with the forest. We shall miss them not for sentimental reasons, but because they constitute a potential source of cultures, medicaments, fibres and new kinds of food. Did you know that maize alone, for example, is used in the manufacture of aspirin, penicillin, paper and plastic materials?

Everywhere we are witnessing (powerless to act?) an unbelievable squandering of resources which, if properly managed, could ensure our subsistence for many more millennia.

*   *   *

We have polluted the Blue Planet, a name it will soon no longer deserve. We have unscrupulously ravaged the Ocean, which Homer described as the father of all the gods. Fresh or salt, water is the 'source of all things', wrote Thales of Miletus. It engenders, vitalises, regenerates and fecundates. The contempt and casualness with which we squander this treasure has much to say about our attitude to life.

For a long time we have reassured ourselves by exaggerating the sea's regenerative capacities. We claimed that it could digest and wash clean all the filth we poured into it: sewage water from towns, effluent from factories, discharges from ships, oilslicks, pesticides and various chemical products swept down by rivers. We have even gone so far as to throw our nuclear waste into the sea, in the vain belief that it would be quite safe there. Today France, the most 'nuclearised' country in the world, simply does not know what to do with its nuclear waste.

There was international concern recently when it was learnt that several nuclear submarines had ended up on the ocean bed. Soviet and American wrecks, which could all represent time-bombs lying off our coasts. The ignorance of sorcerers' apprentices! Countless Russian warships, abandoned because of lack of money for their upkeep, rot away in their home ports, discharging fuel and other toxic waste.

Many regions of the sea are also in danger of dying. Their stocks of fish are no longer renewing themselves, if they are not already unfit for consumption. Ancient traditions say that whales and dolphins were non-terrestrial mammals introduced into our seas by the gods to watch over the state of the planet. What would happen if these intelligent creatures, destroyed by marine toxicity, disappeared?

*

When we are not poisoning the sea, we are over-feeding it. Phosphorus, in the form of phosphate, is not in itself toxic, but it is a hyperfertilising food, an excess of which stimulates a proliferation of algae, leading to a deoxygenation of the water responsible for massive hecatombs of marine and freshwater life. Thus the celebrated red alga *Oscillatoria rubescens*, also called 'Blood of the Burgundians', is gradually stifling many of our lakes. 'And the third part of the sea became blood,' says St John.

Even the water intended for human consumption is being affected. Once again I shall be accused of wanting to sow seeds of panic, but did you know that in many respects the quality of Paris tap water does not meet the standards laid down by the regulations? It has been found to contain five times as many nitrates and pesticide residues as it did 15 years ago. This could result in a marked increase in cancers and infections of the blood. Drinking water in New York has been found to contain traces, higher than those laid down by the World Health Organisation, of aldicarb, a powerful neurotoxin. And so mankind goes on, 'drinking of necessity waters poisoned by sulphur' (Nostradamus, 10th Century, quatrain 49).

This is a planetary phenomenon, involving both countryside and towns. The deepest lake in the world, Lake Baikal, lies in the heart of Siberia. Today this unique ecosystem is a patient on the danger-list, asphyxiated by the waste from cellulose and paper-making factories. Nearly all the prophecies predict that 'There will be a shortage of water one day'.

*

If earth and water are poisoned, our food, too, must be poisoned. Who can foresee the precise effects on our bodies and in particular our neurones of all the toxic substances we are absorbing willy-nilly? Meat contains synthetic hormones, and the insecticides used in agriculture are today associated with leuk-aemia, spontaneous abortions and various nervous diseases. Every year nearly a million people are poisoned by pesticides with outlandish names. Did you know that every morning, when filtering our coffee or using a teabag, we are absorbing quantities (admittedly minute) of dioxin, which is used to whiten paper? Many colourants whose carcinogenic 'properties' have been proved have still not been taken off the market. According to some specialists, most cancers are caused by the deterioration of the environment and the diet we follow . . . No point in rushing to buy organic vegetables: they are just as contaminated, because they grow in the same soil as the others and they are watered from the same sources. In the industrialised countries, we swallow nearly ten grams of chemical additives per kilo of food consumed!

No use going on a strict fast as a precaution: the air we breathe is just as dangerous. Studies carried out on populations living near industrial centres show a dramatic increase in headaches and hormonal dysfunctions.

By attacking our immune system, these toxic substances make us more vulnerable to viruses. Who can say that they are not also contributory factors in those maladies of the modern age, urban aggressiveness, stress and depression? Must we wait until we produce a generation of mutants before we bestir ourselves? The Earth looks like achieving on its own a purification that has become essential.

* * *

Let's stop there. The list of ecological problems now threatening us is too appalling, and I would fill a whole book if I tried to tell you about all the countless sorrows of the Blue Planet. It would be far too depressing.

'The earth mourneth and fadeth away . . . the earth is also defiled under the inhabitants thereof; because they have transgressed the laws, changed the ordinance, broken the everlasting covenant,' Isaiah tells us (24:4—5). Today the fears of Hermes Trismegistus have been proved only too right. He wrote in his *Corpus Hermeticum*:

Men will no longer regard the world as the object worthy of their admiration and their reverence . . . They will despise and no longer cherish the Universe, incomparable work of God, glorious construction. Creation of all goodness made of an infinite diversity of forms, instrument of the will of God who, without envy, lavishes his favour on his work in which is assembled, in a single whole, into a harmonious diversity, everything that can be offered to our regard as worthy of reverence, praise and love . . .

We have forgotten that Gaia, the earth that nurtures us, made up a whole and, more importantly, a living being. Modern man has put himself at a remove from Nature. He has tried to make it an object divorced from himself, so that he could dominate it at will. In so doing he has become blind to the fact that his own survival depends on the harmony he maintains with his own living environment.

The most recent scientific theories, however, seem to be bringing about a genuine revolution in this field. The English writer James Lovelock regards Gaia as a living organism. As such, she has self-regulating systems comparable to the human body's physiological mechanisms for maintaining the conditions necessary for her existence or simply favourable to her development. This means that there is a total symbiosis between the organisms living on Earth and their environment. The simplest and best known example is undoubtedly that of the maintenance of an almost constant level of oxygen. This maintenance depends on a compromise between oxygen consumers such as humans and animals, and the consumers of carbon dioxide such as plants. In Lovelock's view Gaia's system has much in common with the physiology of warm-blooded animals: the atmosphere can be compared to the planet's lungs; the lubricating system, including rivers and oceans, to the circulation of the blood. In a sense living organisms are the Earth's detectors, so that the interactions between the different species control the planet's metabolism. A natural catastrophe such as a volcanic explosion or a tidal wave can temporarily upset this balance—then life sets about the task of restoring it.

In short, the Earth is 'intelligent', something the secret doctrines have always claimed. They are not of course talking of a human intelligence, but of a 'biological' or even a 'cosmic' intelligence. Unfortunately, our unthinking behaviour is dangerously undermining the mechanisms that have allowed Gaia to maintain her stability. In spite of all its self-regulatory capabilities, our ecosystem today finds itself, for the first time in its history, in very real danger, overwhelmed by all the aggression it has suffered. Lovelock does not hesitate to speak of a 'human plague'. But he also issues a warning. Although Gaia is capable of great generosity when she is respected, she can also exact revenge for the mistreatment inflicted on her. Lovelock tells us that it is in mankind's interest to live in harmony with the Earth. Otherwise Gaia will continue to exist, but with a new biosphere that may well have no place for human beings. Vengeance indeed!

*   *   *

How could the Earth bring about this act of vengeance? The scientists, of course, have their version, while the mystics have theirs . . . which we might call more 'animated'. The Blue Planet has four elements that protect it and could become its weapons in its struggle against the human plague. These elements are earth, air, fire and water, represented by the swastika, the gammadion so horribly misused by the Nazis. An Atlantean symbol found from Central America to the Far East, the swastika consists of four gamma-shaped arms which, while revolving round the centre, represent the creative whirlpool, the development of the world around the fixed point, God. Hitler appropriated this symbol, but he reversed the direction of its gyration. From being positive, the rotation became negative and destructive . . .

The four elements of Gaia are served by spirits.

The earth has its Gnomes who, according to tradition, can be visualised as small, mischievous sprites who live underground and guard precious metals. As for the Undines, they reign under water, like the sirens with long fishes' tails. The regions of air are inhabited by the Sylphs, who resemble large birds with enormous wings and slender, graceful bodies. Lastly, the Salamanders, who are like lizards or dwarf dragons. They live in and are nourished by fire.

In a sense these spirits are the soul of things; they represent the protective energies at work in nature. Having no consciences and personalities of their own, they were created solely to ensure the Earth's safety. Normally they do not show themselves and are quite invisible to those who do not believe in their existence, but once in a while they do appear . . .

Last year I was returning from Tokyo by air, sitting next to the window as I always do. While I was looking out, I suddenly heard a most peculiar kind of whistle. Naturally, my first thought was that it came from the engine. I leant forward and, near the end of the wing, I saw a sort of enormous, tapering cloud. All at once the cloud took the form of a bird and flew off with a barely perceptible flapping of its wings.

I know how extraordinary this may sound to the untutored reader. But what we take for inanimate matter does indeed have a soul and hidden lives. Crystals, marine whirlpools, flames, even the breeze, are the refuge and signs of these mysterious beings. When I was a child in Brittany, the farmers still believed that when ploughing a field one must always leave a corner untilled so that the gnomes and fairies of the place could go and dance there. Bachelard claimed that these spirits 'come to us when we call them by their names'. Actually, they are only perceptible to beings who have crossed the bridge that links us with the beyond. To those, in other words, who have retained their capacity for wonder and admiration when looking at the world. After all, is that not what the Bible tells us? 'Except ye . . . become as little children, ye shall not enter into the kingdom of heaven.'

*　*　*

Those kindly spirits the Gnomes could turn themselves into evil spirits. First and foremost their mission was to help mankind, but they could easily rebel against us. To rid itself of human beings, those harmful parasites, the Earth is going to shake its crust. All the prophecies predict terrible earthquakes for us. The seer Giovanni di Vatiguerro wrote in his *Book of Wonders*: 'The earth, struck with fear, will experience terrifying tremors in many places and will swallow up all living things. Many towns, fortresses and strong castles will collapse and be overthrown.' Zechariah (14:4) foretells the opening of a gigantic fault which suggests the parting of the continental plates: '. . . and the mount of Olives shall cleave in the midst thereof toward the east and toward the west; and half of the mountain shall remove toward the north and half of it toward the south.'

Volcanic activity on the earth has never been so strong as during the last twenty-odd years. From the west coast of America to the mountains of the Caucasus, from China to Egypt, never a day passes without a tremor, however faint, being felt in some part of the globe. Sura 67 of the Koran puts this question to us: 'Are you sure that he who is in the heavens will not open the ground under your feet? Already it is trembling.' And Sura 99 adds:

When the earth shall tremble with a violent trembling,

So that she shall have shaken all her burdens,
Man will ask: What has happened to the earth?
Then she will tell what she knows,
That which thy lord shall inspire her to.

The Undines will give the Gnomes a helping hand.
We know that terrestrial catastrophes are followed
by gigantic tidal waves, the formidable *tsunamis*.
People still remember the disaster at Valparaiso in
Chile, in 1952. A wave about 40 metres high broke
over the town, carrying all before it, people and
houses. The driving force behind this wave came
from Siberia, about 15,000 kilometres away.

'The waves of the sea shall travel to distant shores
to put fear into the nations,' says the prophecy of
Prémol. Found in the convent of the same name in
1783, it foretold with extraordinary clarity the
upheavals of French history, in particular the Revolution and the Napoleonic Empire. Giovanni di Vatiguerro (once again) declares that 'The sea will bellow
and rise against the world.'

So what do the scientists say? As a direct consequence of the greenhouse effect, the heating up of
the planet will cause glaciers to melt and an impressive rise in the sea-level. Then regions, islands and
whole countries will be submerged and the waters of
the oceans will flow into each other.

The *Vishnu Purana* also warns us of flooding
rains: 'Gigantic clouds will cover the earth. Then, by
means of an interminable deluge, they will swamp
the whole world with water. This rain will inundate
the earth for twelve years and mankind will be
destroyed. The earth will be like unto one great
ocean.'

Yet Christians should have reason to hope that the
inundations will be limited and that at least part of
the land will remain above the water level. For after
the Flood, God said to Noah: 'And I will establish my

covenant with you; neither shall all flesh be cut off any more by the waters of a flood; neither shall there be any more a flood to destroy the earth.' But the fact remains that we have not respected that covenant, because we have broken the clause that asked us to recognise the Creator as sole master of the world . . . Shall we then see the Undines drown the world?

*

One thing is certain: the Sylphs will prove no more kindly. These delicate beings can transform themselves into implacable enemies. After all, it is the air which carries aircraft! Supposing the Sylphs went on strike? As we have seen, recent years have chalked up a record number of air disasters.

But that is not all the Sylphs could do—far from it. They could summon up tempests and hurricanes. Heating the planet by one degree would double the frequency of cyclones. The Sylphs could also render the earth completely barren by sweeping away and dispersing the fine layer of arable soil that covers it. They could spread radio-active particles over thousands of miles, as happened after the Chernobyl disaster. As rulers of our atmosphere, the Sylphs could stop filtering the ultraviolet rays, so condemning us to die by being virtually roasted. In my dreams I have seen men covered with black patches and burns caused by the sun.

Worst of all, the Sylphs can carry to us all kinds of unknown viruses and toxic products. Giovanni di Vatiguerro tells us:

The air will be infected and corrupted because of the malice and iniquity of men. The natural course of the air will be almost totally changed and perverted because of pestilential maladies. Men, as well as animals, will be stricken by various infirmities, and by sudden death; there will be an unspeakable plague.

Today we humans have an impressive panoply of deadly gases at our disposal. Many accidents have given sufficient proof of that. Just think of what happened at Seveso in 1976 when dioxin, a very deadly poison, was released into the atmosphere. Within the perimeter affected by the toxic cloud, birds fell from the sky, domestic animals died and the place had to be evacuated as a disaster area. Men suffered from terrible tumours. Those most affected were confined to a zone to which access was forbidden. The earth was so impregnated with the poison that it had to be removed by bulldozers—which incidentally proved quite inadequate. There was a dramatic increase in congenital malformations and the people exposed are still the victims of long-term effects. Subsequently we have learnt that drums of dioxin were found in French waste discharges . . .

Then there was Bhopal in 1984. A very volatile gas, methyl isocyanide, escaped from a tank in an insecticide factory. All around thousands of people had their lungs affected and began to vomit blood, while the gas made their eyes burn. It is estimated that this 'accident' caused some 10,000 deaths, not to mention 20,000 sick, and 200,000 people who still suffer from eye infections and stomach pains. Women now experience gynaecological complications and pregnancy problems.

Seveso, Bhopal . . . What will be the third great chemical catastrophe? Today our armed forces possess an unusually powerful gas: two thousandths of a gramme are enough to kill a man, 50 kilogrammes could wipe the population of France off the map. No point in rushing to buy a gasmask: it would be quite useless because some of these products can penetrate the pores of the skin.

St Hildegard, the great twelfth-century prophet-ess, abbess of the Benedictines at Bingen, warned of 'a great cloud which will spread an odour of fright-ful and truly infernal corruption.'

But the Sylphs will never be more powerful than when they join forces with the fire-dwelling Sala-manders.

*

The prophecies are almost unanimous in making fire the chosen instrument of the divine wrath. 'For a fire is kindled in mine anger and shall burn into the lowest hell, and shall consume the earth with her increase,' it is written in Deuteronomy.

The Flood caused the first destruction of the world, flames will be responsible for the second. This belief is found in the most ancient traditions and civilis-ations, from the Atlantic peoples to the Aztec and Amazonian Indians, from Mazdean writings to the Revelation of St John where we see the seventh angel who 'stood at the altar with a golden censer . . . (he) filled it with fire from the altar and threw it on the earth.' Claude Lévi-Strauss quotes a myth of the Ge Indians which says that the Moon stole a diadem of fire from the sun. 'The diadem burnt her hands and she let it drop to earth, the whole savannah caught fire and the animals were consumed.'

The Latin poet Lucan also expressed this fear: 'Fire will destroy the world, nothing will escape the fury of the flames on the day when earth and sky shall fuse into a single blazing mass.'

The sources of this mighty conflagration could be many and various. We have already raised the possi-bility of a meteorite strike which could cause spon-taneous fires at the four corners of the globe by rapidly raising the temperature of the atmosphere. Or it might slightly change the Earth's orbit, thus exposing it dangerously to the Sun's merciless rays.

But the greatest risks are closer to home. For example, we know the consequences of turning the Mediterranean forests into brushwood. In one generation the area of France ravaged by fire has trebled. We may also recall the gigantic fire which blazed furiously in the Rocky Mountains of America. It seems that the Salamanders have never been so busy . . .

But we ourselves are not far behind! The fires caused by our murderous folly can no longer be counted. Since Vietnam, we know all about the action of napalm bombs. Today we possess phosphorus bombs that burn even on bare rock. Many prophecies proclaim the destruction of the great capital cities by the fires of war. This is how St Caesarius of Arles (470—542) describes the end of Paris: 'Fire and iron envelop the Babylon of Gaul which falls in a vast fire.'

Undoubtedly, the most terrifying is still atomic fire which, in all probability, will play a crucial role. It is strange to find a premonition of it in a seventeenth-century text known as the Prophecy of the Unknown Monk: 'Burning rays, more burning than the most incandescent sun, moving iron fortresses and flying vessels full of terrible bullets and arrows, deadly shooting stars and sulphurous fire will destroy the great towns.' Could there be a better description of nuclear weapons, assault tanks, giant bombers and the missiles that form our modern armadas?

The incandescent fire could also refer to the neutron bomb which liberates its energy in the form of rays capable of passing through walls and metal like an arrow through a net. Neutrons disintegrate body cells and then the body becomes virtually liquefied: 'Your breath, as fire, shall devour you,' we read in Isaiah (33:11 and 12), 'And the people shall be as the burnings of lime: as thorns cut up shall they be burned in the fire.'

And surely this nuclear apocalypse is also to be

found in St John? He tells us (Rev. 8:10–11) of 'a great star . . . burning as it were a lamp, and it fell upon the third part of the rivers, and upon the fountains of waters; And the name of the star is called Wormwood: and the third part of waters became wormwood; and many men died of the waters, because they were made bitter.' I have already mentioned in my previous book that the word 'Wormwood' is translated into Ukrainian as a name that resounds like a trumpet of the Apocalypse: Chernobyl.

Because it contaminates earth and water, because it is both a fire and an invisible threat that disperses itself in the atmosphere, the nuclear catastrophe seems to represent a destructive alliance of Gnomes, Undines, Sylphs and Salamanders.

When nuclear power stations were first being built, we all heard the leading experts assure us that the chances of an accident were no more than one in a billion. Today we already have three on record: Kyshtyn in 1957, Three Mile Island in 1979 and Chernobyl in 1986, not to mention other less serious incidents. How could we be so gullible? Confronted with the evidence, the scientists have revised their odds. Many of them now put the chances of a major nuclear accident between now and the end of the century at fifty-fifty.

In short, it is no longer a question of how to prevent similar accidents, but how 'best' to live through them. At the beginning of this chapter I expressed the fear that we have reached the point of no return . . .

* * *

Does this mean that the Earth is going to cease to exist? I sincerely hope not. Nevertheless, we cannot exclude the worst of scenarios. Everything that is born must die, and the Earth will not escape this rule. We know that our Sun is not immortal and that its life expectancy is estimated at some five billion years, which leaves us time to wait and see. Obviously the annihilation of the Sun will mean the Earth's destruction. But it will still not be the end of the world. The explosion of this star will make way for other planets, other stars. The vast cosmic cycle will begin again. I am convinced that the distant galaxies contain thousands of inhabited and developed constellations which will take over from us.

In the visions inspired by my astral journeys I have had the intuition of another planet, called Traïa, that must have been the first laboratory of civilisation in our galaxy. On this planet, situated between Mars and Jupiter, the Elohim, those ancient gods mentioned in the Hebraic Bible, made the first attempt at human colonisation. Traïa developed, the inhabitants multiplied, but they finally rebelled and turned away from their creators. Caught up in its ascension to a higher Vibratory Plane, Traïa exploded some five billion years ago, causing bombardments of asteroids, traces of which remain on all the planets of our solar system. These are the craters we see on Mercury, Venus, Mars and the Moon. And some of those stellar bodies combined to form the girdle of asteroids around Jupiter, the gaseous planet.

Long after this failure, the Elohim, inspired by the Divinity, tried out a new experiment on Earth (we shall return to this in the next chapter). Today we are at the same crucial turning-point that Traïa could not handle. If the Earth cannot rise on the vibratory scale, it will be threatened with explosion. If the vibratory rate of the Cosmos is too high and that of the Earth too low, there is bound to be rupture. Much as a crystal glass shatters when subjected to a very strong musical note because it is unable to rise in the chromatic scale.

But we have not reached that stage yet. I look on

the Apocalypse that haunts us as more like a purification effected by Gaia. The Earth will shake itself to get rid of the toxic products injected by the human plague. It will not be a final destruction, but a restructuring and a Renaissance before a new Age.

* * *

What will happen then? If we cannot take the planet with us, might we disappear from the face of the earth? Unfortunately I think that that is quite possible. 'We others, the civilised races, know now that we are mortal,' said Valéry. Since then we have moved up a notch: we now know that it is the whole human race that is mortal. The age of the dinosaurs has returned, the age of man could give place to the age of the insects, whose resistance to changes of temperature and high levels of radioactivity is well known.

The most plausible scenario, however, is that although the Earth will eliminate a large section of humanity, a part will survive. 'Many shall be purified, and made white and tried,' Daniel tells us.

'But they that shall escape of them shall escape, and shall be on the mountains like doves of the valleys, all of them mourning, every one for his iniquity.' (Ezek. 7:16.)

And Isaiah (26:20—21):

Come, my people, enter thou into thy chambers, and shut thy doors about thee: hide thyself as it were for a little moment, until the indignation be overpast. For, behold, the Lord cometh out of his place to punish the inhabitants of the earth for their iniquity.

The Revelation of St John also has something to say about those who will be saved (7:2—4):

He cried with a loud voice to the four angels, to whom it was given to hurt the earth and the sea . . . saying, Hurt not the earth, neither the sea, nor the trees, till we have sealed the servants of our God in their foreheads. And I heard the number of them which were sealed: and there were sealed an hundred and forty and four thousand of all the tribes of the children of Israel.

Theirs would be the mission of rebuilding the Earth. At first they might lead a precarious existence, but the Knowledge would be preserved. After all, it would not be the first time in the history of the world that such tribulations have suddenly been inflicted on mankind . . .

Chapter 3

THE SURVIVORS OF ATLANTIS

Imagination is the queen of truth, and the possible is one of her provinces.

Baudelaire

What do we really know about our history? I am not talking about our recent history, which roughly covers the age of Pisces. That is comparatively well known. It is, however, no more than the tip of an enormous iceberg. Have we any conception of the peaks and gulfs hidden beneath the modest level of our proven knowledge? While a student at the Beaux Arts, I was fascinated by these whole areas of our past that remain unexplored, as if lost in the mists of time. What remains of the saga of those ancient peoples, builders of civilisations that shone so brilliantly many millennia before our own?

What do we really know about the 'History before History'? Very little, we have to admit. How many shadowy areas, how many unsolved enigmas hide the true face of our forebears from us? Admittedly, archaeological discoveries are constantly pushing back the bounds of our knowledge. For some two centuries now, there have been spectacular upsets to shake our perception of antiquity and prehistory. Excavations in South America and Mesopotamia (the Fertile Crescent) have revealed traces of cities we had no idea existed. Or rather, we doubted their existence, our only evidence being a few ancient texts or simply oral tradition. To give just one example, we know that the city of Troy was long thought to be a purely legendary site, born of the imagination of the author of the *Iliad*. But in 1870, when Heinrich Schliemann, working from the Homeric poems, discovered traces of successive settlements on the coasts of the Hellespont, the truth had to be faced: the Trojan War did in fact take place!

Cities have been salvaged from the sand at Jericho in Israel, at Çatal Hüyük in Turkey and Lagash in Iraq. They prove that highly organised civilisations were developed long before the dates which we had previously fixed as the starting point for the birth of humanity. These civilisations knew their hour of glory, then they perished, leaving no clue to the real reason for their sudden decline. The discovery in Peru and Colombia of almost intact but completely abandoned cities gives us the strange feeling that they had been abruptly deserted by their inhabitants, fleeing before some cataclysm now quite forgotten by history. Basically, these lost civilisations illustrate the inescapable law of cycles: birth, development, apogee and death. That was their destiny, and it could be ours. In short, they remind us that it is not impossible that we too shall sink into oblivion one day . . .

*

In two of his dialogues, *Timaeus* and *Critias*, Plato recalls the figure of Solon (640–558 BC), an important Athenian politician reputed for his reforming zeal. This sage of ancient Greece was also a great traveller, especially to Egypt. There he was able to hold long conversations with the country's wisest priests. One of them spoke to him in words that could equally well have been addressed to us:

> You Hellenes, your minds are still like children's
> . . . because you have no ancient opinion based
> on an old tradition and no science grown white

with age. And this is why. The destruction of mankind, caused in various ways, has happened many times and will often happen again.

Then the Egyptian priests told Solon that this ancient Tradition had been stored in secret hiding places in their temples from time immemorial and that the documents in their possession clearly described the destruction of an island, the size of a continent, which they called Atlantis.

These writings mentioned a people 'coming from another world situated in the Atlantic Ocean. In those days it was possible to cross the ocean, because there was an island opposite the strait that you call the pillars of Heracles.'

These pillars of Heracles, or Hercules, are what we now call the Straits of Gibraltar.

'This island was bigger than Libya and Asia put together,' continued the Egyptian priests. 'From it one could pass on to the other islands and from them reach the whole continent which extends in front of them and lines this great sea.'

So if we are to believe Plato, the Egyptians knew of the existence of the Caribbean Islands and America stituated beyond Atlantis.

But this Atlantean kingdom was suddenly engulfed. 'There were extraordinary earthquakes and floods,' Solon was told. 'In the space of a single day and a single night of ill fortune, the Island of Atlantis was swallowed up by the sea and disappeared without a trace.'

The mysterious continent was wiped out, taking a whole civilisation into the realm of legend. And if Atlantis interests us today, it is because it possibly prefigures what we ourselves are soon to experience: the end of an era.

What had happened? What was the origin of this highly developed people? How and why had the island sunk with all hands? Or did it somehow manage to prolong its influence in one form or another? The replies to these questions could throw light on our past and on our future.

Fascinated and guided by Plato's account, many explorers have tried to discover the remains of Atlantis. Some 2,000 kilometres west of Spain there is a high underwater plateau that could be the sunken continent. Some of its crests, such as the Ampere peak, level off only 70 metres from the surface of the sea. The rest of the plateau lies at a depth of up to 2,500 metres. Samples of rock taken there show the presence of dead coral. Since coral cannot start to grow at such a depth, it would seem to indicate that this region was once much higher and that it suddenly sank. Only a few points of the lost continent remain above water: they are the islands of the Azores and Madeira, the Cape Verde Islands, and the Bermudas and the Bahamas off the coast of America.

In 1969 divers at Bimini, off the Bahamas, made a discovery that excited the whole scientific world, as well as everyone interested in the mystery of Atlantis. They had found a causeway several hundred metres long by ten metres wide, made of enormous blocks of stone. This giant roadway was certainly not of natural origin, as the precise arrangement of the stones showed, and the way they were cut at right angles. Everything suggested that it was a highway, perhaps a royal road that plunged beneath the sea and the sand in the supposed direction of Atlantis.

Megalithic structures that have long intrigued fishermen and oceanographers have been found in many parts of the region known as the Bermuda Triangle. Airline pilots flying over this part of the sea have also observed formations like city walls or underwater roads. In spite of their geometric designs (stone circles and straight lines) they had long been interpreted as natural formations, but the Bimini discovery put paid to that theory. Could they be the remains of Atlantean ports or colonies engulfed by the great cataclysm that destroyed the mother island?

Edgar Cayce, a celebrated American clairvoyant who died in 1945, claimed to have visions through hypnotically induced sleep. Twenty-eight years before this archaeological discovery he had declared that Atlantis would reappear around 1969—not far from the Island of Bimini. In 1929 he also predicted that in about a hundred years' time, after a series of earthquakes, islands would rise from the ocean in the region of the Azores and that the ruins of Atlantis would be discovered and explored.

Perhaps Cayce had read these lines by Seneca:

> A time will come in the world's old age
> When the ocean will free what it hides away
> And a land will appear in all its glory.

Meanwhile, the peoples and the geographic names all round the borders of this ocean seem to send back echoes of the sunken continent: Atlas, Antilles, Andes, Andalusia . . . As for the Aztecs, they claim that their name is derived from that of the mountainous island from which they came and which they now look on as their paradise lost: *Aztlan.*

*

The archaeologists, for their part, still hesitate to confirm the existence of Atlantis, perhaps because, if they did, they would be forced to rewrite the whole history of mankind. Until conclusive proof is provided, they intend to wait and see. Their rigorous scholarship does them credit. But we should take care that their cool detachment does not lead us to reject the possibilities out of hand. For some time now, I have noted with interest some progress in scientific attitudes. Now Atlantis is no longer looked on as a myth without foundation, but as a working hypothesis.

What does it matter, after all? One thing is sure: there are still too many unknown quantities in our history for anyone to think he has the real truth and to dismiss all other claims as nonsense. Little by little we are breaking new ground, and yesterday's certainties often give way to question marks. Our knowledge does not stand still, it is continually correcting itself in order to recapture the thread of our Great History. Archaeological excavations seem to us to be the signposts in this process, in the same way that the Atlantic archipelagos are the only peaks still above water of what was once a vast continent. Why not try to use these signposts in order to re-establish a bridge with the past? Human advances are guided and stimulated by imagination, quite as much as by empiricism. Men of science are themselves well aware how much their discoveries owe to intuition. So why refuse to plunge into these unknown depths? If all we were to find was the legend, it would be no less rich in information . . .

*

The pages that follow could actually be read as a very beautiful legend, the Story of Mankind. But are not myths essentially poetic versions of reality and the best answers to our enigmas?

Let's look at the crucial question of the origin of mankind. We know that the scientific theories of evolution come up against the major obstacle of the missing link. How could a living cell have been born in a purely mineral world? Today people are challenging the theory by which the meeting of a certain number of gases at a given temperature could have acted as catalysts: the gaseous combination proposed is simply impossible.

For my part, when I state my firm belief that human beings appeared through the intervention of a cosmic power, I am doing no more than agreeing with the most ancient myths in our culture, which form the basis of our religion. But legends speak with many voices. We can take them literally or see them as a vivid way of describing a physical reality. When it comes down to it, you see, my vision is not so far removed from the latest scientific theories, for today it is being suggested that meteorites fallen from the sky brought the first spark of life to Earth. Coming from planets on which a rudimentary form of life existed (but why not a developed form as on Traïa?), these meteorites were the bearers of certain cells or molecules. After being 'stranded' on our mineral planet, these alien elements are said to have given birth to the first living organisms and then to mankind at the culmination of a vast process of combination and evolution. Such a theory would make us 'extra' terrestrials, on the basis of our distant origin.

The point of this preamble is to explain that you should not be surprised when you find here my personal visions intermingled with ancient myths and scientific discoveries. After all, the aim of the game is surely to reveal the meaning of life, without hesitating to use all the tools at our disposal.

At all events, I should be satisfied if the reader (even with tongue in cheek) would agree to set aside for a moment his compartmentalised view of history and envisage the vast destiny of humankind as a whole; if recalling former civilisations could make him adopt a more relative stance towards the basis of his so-called certainties. Lastly, I should be happy if, in the light of this fresco of myth unfolding before him, he could perceive that we are the inheritors of a long human chain with roots stretching back into the mists of time. Perhaps that would lead him to ask himself about the nature of our responsibility in relation to our ancestors and our successors. For we have reached the point where we are in danger of breaking that chain through our own thought-lessness.

* * *

Like my memories and my visions, my reading has led me to think that the centre of our galaxy contains a civilisation that is many billions of years old. Its destiny is presided over by the Sages of Sirius and Orion, invisible governors who rule over many other stars in our galactic system.

After the failure of the Traïa experiment that I men-tioned earlier, these Sages became interested in the planet Earth. As the Earth is situated on one of the outer branches of the galaxy, it forms an ideal bridge-head for possible expeditions to neighbouring nebulae.

The representatives of this distant civilisation are the Elohim, a word that the Hebraic Bible often uses to refer to ancient gods or supernatural beings. Mil-lions of years ago these Elohim approached our planet. They studied it when it was still in a semi-wild state and, five million years ago, obeying the instructions of the Sages of Orion and Sirius, they arrived on Earth to create an amphibian of humanoid appearance from a terrestrial embryo.

Recently I was surprised to learn that the Austra-lian aborigines have a myth explaining the appear-ance of man upon Earth, which is uncannily similar to my own beliefs. They say that in the beginning there were living forms that floated on the muddy water of the marshes. Lacking distinct features such as ears and eyes, these beings resembled translucent globes on which one could just make out the faint outline of limbs and a head. At that point, celestial creatures, whom the aborigines called Ungambikula (our Elohim?), stepped in to model a face with a human appearance. They designed the eyes, mouth and ears. Then came the limbs, and the resulting prehominids left the watery element for the land. As their limbs were still not very strong, they began by creeping like reptiles. Later they began to walk.

Don't we find in this story, in mythical but spectacular form, the same evolutionist theories we are told by our scientists?

*

But let us go back to the Elohim. After producing amphibian creatures, they left planet Earth, but somewhat carelessly without completing the evolutionary process.

Some 78,000 years ago, judging that the time was ripe, the Sages of Sirius and Orion gave the Elohim the mission of returning to Earth to organise the first human civilisation. So they set off, accompanied by scholars and other instructors recruited from many planets in our galaxy.

When they arrived on the Blue Planet, the Great Instructors found to their consternation that the specimens abandoned to their fate had not always developed as intended. Indeed, as a result of various genetic aberrations, the humanoids had given birth to a number of mutants, whose existence has been preserved in ancient legends. Some of them were half-man, half-horse and some half-man, half-bull, whom the Greeks called Centaurs and Bucentaurs. There were men with jackals' heads, like the Egyptian Anubis. And Harpies with women's bodies, but with wings and talons; sirens with long fishes' tails; satyrs with he-goats' hooves and horns; werewolves . . . The Elohim also found fabulous beasts, such as griffins, with the beak and wings of eagles and with a lion's body; gorgons, their heads wreathed with snakes, their mouths full of wild boars' tusks;

winged horses like Pegasus; chimeras with lions' heads, goats' bodies and dragons' tails, who spat flames . . .

Is it so strange to believe that these monsters that we have preserved in the depths of our unconscious are not gratuitous inventions? Does not the fact that they recur, with symbolic differences, in the myths and legends of many peoples suggest that these hybrid creatures actually existed in very remote times? While still a child, I had absolutely no doubt that centaurs and unicorns could have been seen in the flesh in the distant past. Before being reborn in our fancies, these amazing creatures must have been alive! Has not palaeontology revealed to us that equally monstrous reptilians left their imprints on the dawn of time?

Be that as it may, aghast at the aberrant course taken by the evolution of human and animal life, the envoys from Sirius and Orion must have set about a vast purification process. They sacrificed many species in order to put mankind back on the right path.

In so doing, the Elohim and their assistants forgot one important detail. While suppressing the 'monsters', they shed a lot of blood. So our Great Instructors shouldered a heavy karma for their criminal deeds. In their desire to work for the good of humanity, they committed acts against life. This karma must have bound them to the fate of the Earth for millennia. Thereafter, at the end of each of their existences, they must have returned to our planet in successive reincarnations to wash themselves clean of this first pogrom—never mind that its victims had been hybrid monsters, never mind that its only purpose had been the foundation of a genuinely human civilisation . . .

Gradually the Great Instructors found themselves becoming inextricably linked to planet Earth. They married humans and ultimately forgot about their distant origin. In Genesis it is said that the sons of God (the Elohim) 'saw the daughters of men that they were fair; and they took them wives of all which they chose'. Then they gave birth to the Nephilim, the giants we find in all the legends. These giants may have had some connection with the cyclopean structures of the earliest times, from the ruins of Sacsahuaman in Peru to the colossal statues to be found on Easter Island and in Ancient Egypt. Then those Titanesque creatures, the Nephilim, must have disappeared in their turn, so that confusion and inequality ceased and Earth finally came to exist with man as the measure of things.

* * *

Elsewhere I have described how I had the sudden revelation of my first incarnation on Earth. One day in my present life, during a chance meeting with three strangers, I suddenly had a strong feeling that I had known them before. A long time ago . . . Strange images jostled about in my mind, confirmed by similar sensations experienced by the others. Then a 'truth' forced itself upon me, the truth of my first origin.

I came from the 'crystal' planet in the constellation of the Eagle which orbits around the star Altair. Was I, along with these three individuals, part of the expedition organised by the Elohim to civilise the Earth? That is my firm personal conviction, which nothing can shake. The confused images of that cosmic voyage form my earliest memories, which I can date to about 78,000 years ago. Later I was one of the legislators who banded together to give birth to the Atlantean civilisation. As an accomplice in massacring the hybrid monsters, I thenceforth had to link my destiny with that of the planet Gaia . . .

* * *

When the Elohim had completed their vast task of cleaning up the terrestrial menagerie, the foundations were laid. *Homo sapiens* had just made his appearance. He was to conquer the world.

Under the guidance of the Great Instructors, four civilisations emerged. For a long time they lived in harmony, or in ignorance of each other (I don't know which) in the four corners of the globe.

The kingdom of Thule occupied the northern part of our hemisphere. Its inhabitants, the Hyperboreans, who lived 'beyond the north wind', were a white race. They are mentioned in both Scandinavian and oriental traditions. Thule is none other than the Celtic Avalon or the Hindu Varahi: the primordial home of *Homo sapiens*.

The kingdom of Mu, headquarters of the yellow race, was implanted in the Pacific Ocean. This enormous kingdom extended from south-east Asia to the west coast of the present-day American continent. Most of Mu has disappeared, swallowed up by the waters, like Atlantis. The only remains of this continent are the Indonesian islands and the myriad archipelagos of the Pacific.

Africa constituted the kingdom of Gondwana, cradle of the black race.

Lastly, 'beyond the Pillars of Hercules' in the middle of the Atlantic Ocean, arose the civilisation of the Atlanteans, the most developed of the four. The Atlanteans were called the Red Men because of their copper-coloured skin. Many millennia later, when the Spaniards set foot on the American continent, some strange intuition made them call the inhabitants, the heirs of the Atlanteans, 'Redskins'.

Atlantis flourished rapidly. Handicrafts, then the arts and finally science and technology developed under the tutelage of the Great Instructors, whose karma had condemned them to the role of permanent guides.

Plato gives a precise description of the irresistible expansion of this civilisation:

On the island of Atlantis, the kings had formed a great and admirable power. Its dominance extended over the whole island and many other isles, and some parts of the continent. Moreover, beyond the straits, on our side, they held sway from Libya to Egypt, and from Europe to the Tyrrhenian Sea.

The Atlanteans put all their knowledge into the construction of vast and complex buildings and built the most grandiose of capitals:

With all the wealth they extracted from the earth the inhabitants built temples, the kings' palaces, ports and maritime shipyards, and they embellished all the rest of the country in the order that I shall describe. They began by building bridges over the seawater channels that surrounded the ancient metropolis in order to provide an access to the outside and to the royal palace. They had originally built this palace on the site inhabited by the God and by their ancestors. Each king, on inheriting it from his predecessor, added to its embellishments and took great pains to surpass him, so that they made their dwelling an object of admiration by the grandeur and beauty of their works. From the sea to the outside enclosure, they dug a channel three plethra wide, one hundred feet deep and fifty stadia long, and for vessels coming from the sea they created an entrance into this channel, as if into a harbour, by making an opening big enough for the largest ships to pass through.

To decorate their monuments, the Atlanteans used the most precious metals, regardless of expense, including some the composition of which we no longer know, such as orichalc. The custom of covering temple walls with gold-leaf is also found in later civilisations, the Babylonian and Inca, for example. The Egyptian pyramids were originally covered with sheets of this precious metal, which generations of robbers persisted in dismantling. Plato goes on:

> The whole of the outside of the temple was faced with silver, apart from the acroteria [roof ornaments], which were clad with gold. Inside, the whole vault was of ivory enamelled with gold, silver and orichalc. Everything else, walls, columns and pavements, was ornamented with orichalc. Gold statues were erected there, especially the statue of the God, standing in a chariot, driving six winged horses and so tall that his head touched the vault, then, in a circle around him, a hundred nereids riding dolphins . . . Around the outside of the temple stood gold statues of all the princesses and all the princes who were descended from the ten kings, and many more great statues dedicated by the kings and private citizens, either from the town itself or from the foreign countries subject to their authority.

A civilisation displaying such splendour and such an arrogant will to conquer must inevitably have known hard-fought internecine wars. Soon came the first incidents, then the first armed conflicts between human beings.

Thenceforth two parties disputed control of the kingdom: the sons of Belial and the sons of the One. The former were polytheists, the latter believed in a single God. The monotheists thought that Atlantean society should continue to base itself on the values of the Tradition. The sons of Belial, on the other hand, were innovators in the worst sense of the word, rationalists who had forgotten their divine cosmic origin and wanted to exercise to the full their power over the world.

Were not these rivalries inherent in what was now the obviously human nature of the Atlanteans? That is what Plato suggests when he describes the spiritual decadence which is oddly reminiscent of our own:

> For many generations, as long as the nature of the god sufficed to inspire them, the Atlanteans remained obedient to the voice of his laws and favourably disposed with regard to the divine foundation of their mutual relationship . . . But when the lot they held from god began to tarnish in them through having mingled, oft-times, with many a mortal element, when the human character predominated in them, thenceforth, powerless to bear the weight of their present condition, they lost all propriety in their mode of conduct and their moral ugliness was revealed to eyes capable of seeing it, because among the most precious of goods they had lost those which are the most beautiful.

Under the influence of the Sons of Belial, the science of the Atlanteans was gradually perverted. In their deluded self-importance, these apprentice sorcerers even tried to transform the planet and especially to modify its climate, which was slowly cooling. To this end, they tried to manipulate its telluric forces. Just like the human body, the Earth is crisscrossed by electromagnetic currents. To mark out the location of these fields of force and then act on them, the Sons of Belial erected giant stones. We can still see the relics of their operations in the famous standing stones at Stonehenge and Carnac. All these alignments, as well as the immense straight lines like landing strips to be found at Nazca in Peru, were intended to reverse the magnetic fields. Even today these menhir sites are looked on as evil places in the collective memory of peoples all over the world.

Then what was bound to happen did happen. The manipulations of the Sons of Belial caused Atlantis to be swallowed up. Reversal of the magnetic fields was intended to make the climate warmer, but in fact its first consequence was a modification of the axis of the earth's rotation, which produced terrible seismic shocks.

This 'displacement of the earth's axis' finds a strange echo in a legend of the Hopi Indians, an Amerindian tribe, which relates that the North and South Poles were guarded by two pairs of twins and that when the Creator wanted to destroy the world to make room for another, he simply ordered two guards to abandon their post . . .

The Sons of Belial succeeded beyond their wildest dreams! The entire planet began to warm up, and ice, melting on a massive scale, helped to swell the tidal waves provoked by the telluric shock. The Sons of Belial had just condemned Atlantis to destruction.

All this happened about 12,000 years ago—that is, at the moment of transition from the age of Virgo, the sign of organisation, to the age of Leo, the sign of the power of nature. And this is the same dating that has been scientifically ascribed to the biblical Flood.

*   *   *

It is written in Genesis 6:

And God saw that the wickedness of man was great in the earth and that every imagination of the thoughts of his heart was only evil continu-ally . . . And the Lord said, I will destroy man

> whom I have created from the face of the earth
> . . . And, behold, I, even I, do bring a flood of
> waters upon the earth, to destroy all flesh,
> wherein is the breath of life . . . and everything
> that is in the earth shall die.

Many have chosen to interpret this universal deluge
as a simple myth serving to illustrate God's wrath at
the transgressing of his laws by men. Today, however, we know for certain that the Flood really did
take place, and we can even put a date to it. The
excavations at Ur of the Chaldees (in present-day
Iraq), for example, have enabled archaeologists to
confirm the presence of a layer of mud several metres
thick, the product of alluvial deposits and marine
sedimentations. After Carbon 14 testing, the ceramics found immediately below this layer have
yielded a pretty accurate date for the gigantic inun-
dation: it happened some twelve thousand years ago.

The geologists, for their part, have been able to
establish that the last glaciation began about 80,000
years ago, that is to say, at the period when the Atlantean civilisation began. The Wurm glaciation, as it
was called, experienced several 'bursts' of cold. The
last, about 13,000 years ago, was also the most
intense. Was it the one that so worried the Sons of
Belial? Gigantic glaciers formed, causing a drop in
the sea-level of about 150 metres. At that time the
face of the planet was very different from what it is
today. Can you imagine that England, France, Ire-
land and Scandinavia formed a vast continuous
expanse; that the mouth of the Rhine was somewhere in Norway; that the islands in the Aegean Sea
were attached to Greece; that Saint Malo, La Rochelle
and Lisbon were 200 kilometres inland?

Before them, in the middle of the ocean, rose the
Island of Atlantis, then at its height as a colonial
power. The Atlanteans had established ports to the

east, on the coasts of Spain and Africa, but also to the west, on the Caribbean islands which were separated only by narrow channels. But the ancient towns and their human populations, who had naturally chosen to inhabit these coastal regions, must be sought underwater today, as at Bimini.

Now the final period of the Wurm glaciation was followed 12,000 years ago by a marked warming of the climate. Was it caused by a change in the earth's axis, as I propose? At all events, geologists agree that this global warming was extremely rapid, like lightning on the geological scale. The melting of the ice was accompanied by heavy evaporation and hence by abundant rainfall. The rise in sea-level, the swollen rivers, in addition to the movement of the continental plates, all unleashed a formidable hydraulic activity. Landslides, submerging of coastal land, rivers of mud and flooding destroyed villages, regions and even whole civilisations. That was the enormous cataclysm, the unheard-of catastrophe which has been preserved in the biblical account of the Flood . . .

*

And not only in the Bible! Few themes are as universal as that of the Flood. Indeed, submersion on such a scale was bound to be recorded in every civilisation. The memory of it is found in Indian sacred books, but also in ancient Chinese and Oceanic accounts, not to mention African legends.

Moreoever, was not the Bible itself inspired by older texts? The first written narration of the Flood appears on Sumerian tablets discovered during the excavations of the ruins of the town of Nippur in Iraq. The tablets relate how the gods took the decision to destroy mankind. They unleashed waters and wind with terrible violence for seven days and seven nights. This text later became the source of the Babylonian version of the Flood, as we can read

in the *Epic of Gilgamesh*. In India, Mesopotamia and
Greece, all the ancient civilisations have preserved
the memory of the Flood 'which put an end to
mankind'.

Or, more accurately, which wiped out a civilisation. Because mankind survived. We know that one
man at least (or a group of individuals) escaped the
deluge. Depending on the tradition, this man bore
different names. To the Sumerians he was Ziusudra,
to the Babylonians Um-Napishtim. The Indians
called him Manu and the Greeks Deucalion. And of
course the biblical survivor was Noah.

Regardless of the name he was given, this man
was warned of the coming Flood by God, who gave
him full instructions about how to build the big ship
that would enable him to escape the opening of the
divine flood-gates (Gen. 6:18—19):

> And thou shalt come into the ark, thou, and thy
> sons, and thy wife, and thy son's wives with
> thee. And of every living thing of all flesh, two of
> every sort shalt thou bring into the ark, to keep
> them alive with thee; they shall be male and
> female.

It seems pointless to dwell on the physical impossi-
bility of an undertaking whose aim was to store
examples of all terrestrial fauna and flora aboard a
single ship—even if it was a three-decked one, as Genesis tells us. I think that there is no need here to take
the biblical story literally. I find it hard to imagine one
old man with a hammer building, in record time, a
boat that would withstand the diluvial tidal wave.

So what other theory (or theories) can we suggest?
Did the Elohim, anticipating the culpable actions of
the Sons of Belial, decide to save some of the inhabitants of Atlantis, as well as some from the kingdoms
of Thule, Mu and Gondwana, by putting them in a

safe place? One may well imagine that only the Great Instructors had the means to accomplish the titanic task of saving all the species represented on Earth.

But another question arises. What was done later with these human, animal and vegetable species? It is possible and probable that the Flood spared certain mountainous regions. In that case, the handfuls of survivors could have found refuge in caves, taking a big step backwards in the process. Another interpretation attracts me, because it confirms my meditative visions. The Elohim took Noah's companions to the constellation of Orion and Sirius on board enormous sealed vessels (Arks), until the turmoil of the deluge had quietened down . . .

It was a gnostic reading of the Bible that made me believe in this intervention by the Elohim. The name Noah was formerly read as Noé, and still is in French. This name does not seem to have been chosen by chance. It is a sign. Reading these three letters backwards, one gets 'Eon'. In Greek the word means 'that which exists from all eternity'. For the Hellenes, as for the gnostics, the Eons are eternal powers emanating from the supreme Being. They represent the tutelary gods, the energies through which God is able to exercise his sway over the world. In this respect, Buddha and Jesus Christ are Eons. The name Noé tells us that this man too could be the terrestrial manifestation of an Eon, and not just a 'simple' human being. Something, incidentally, that might explain the apparent lack of interest shown by the Noé of Genesis in the terrible fate of humanity . . .

Noé-Eon, then, would be a divine entity coming from the centre of the Galaxy, sent in emergency by the Sages of Sirius and Orion to save what could be saved. Those who found favour with God would be helped, led to a transit planet, and possibly initiated into certain arcane knowledge.

Later Noé-Eon sent a raven to Earth to make sure

that the planet had recovered its equilibrium. In our legendary hypothesis it is possible that the raven was not a bird, but a kind of reconnaissance mission by the Elohim before the return of the survivors from Atlantis.

Today science, too, has taken up the notion of eons. They are used to designate the invisible elements contained in matter. In more picturesque language, they are the hidden soul of things. So we find the latest Nobel Prizewinner for physics believing that eons would make it possible to recapture the ancient memory locked up in ceramics. Like a long-playing record, a pot formed on the potter's wheel would contain information about the moment of its manufacture.

As you will see, a common denominator, that of everlastingness, is beginning to emerge through all these interpretations. It does not really matter whether Noé existed or not, nor how mankind was saved after the Flood. What counts is the message transmitted by the symbol Noé-Eon. In my opinion, the Bible makes us aware of the permanence of mankind, considered not only as a mere collection of human beings, but also as a transcendental value or 'spirit'—the one brought by the Dove? Each being contains the whole of humanity, 'humantide' as some thinkers put it today. Noé-Eon is the symbol of this continuity of the human race on earth, a continuity guaranteed by God, whatever disasters may strike a corrupt civilisation.

*　　*　　*

We know very little about what happened to humanity after the Flood and the destruction of Atlantis. Were they put into quarantine in the Galaxy until calm reigned again on Earth? Did some groups of surviving Atlanteans turn themselves into troglodytes? The question needs answering.

What we do know, however, is that Sumer, the next civilisation, dates to about 6,000 years ago. That means that there is a gap of six millennia between the Flood and the appearance of an organised post-diluvian civilisation in Mesopotamia! Six thousand years during which the Earth seems to have been almost unoccupied, men being absent or plunged into a cultural regression following the global submersion. Never has the thread of the history of mankind been as tenuous as during this period of darkness.

Archaeology seems to confirm this long hiatus in human development. We know, for instance, that the Magdalenians, who inhabited the area from the Alps to the Cantabrian mountains in Spain, reached their apogee between 15000 BC and the approximate period of the Flood. The paintings at Lascaux and Altamira, near Santander (home-town of my maternal grandfather) bear clear witness to their fertile imagination and the brilliance of their inspiration. One only has to see the extraordinary multicoloured cave paintings at Altamira to be convinced of the Magdalenians' artistic genius. Such an explosion of creativity would certainly be one of the most astonishing events in our history, except for one fact. The people responsible for these paintings were neighbours of Atlantis. Might not their pictorial techniques have been acquired during visits to Atlantean colonies?

But the Magdalenians suddenly disappeared, no doubt swept away by the same cataclysm that engulfed Atlantis. The splendour of their art was to have no equivalent until the arrival of the ancient Egyptian empire, 7,000 years later.

Six millennia . . . Three 'months' in the precessional year. That was the duration of the long silence of humanity, covering the three zodiacal ages of Leo, Cancer and Gemini. Significantly enough, that triad corresponds to the mythological period of Kronos, which signalled a break in evolution for the purpose of restoring order, and preceded the emergence of a genuine self-awareness.

* * *

'History begins at Sumer', the historians tell us. That is both true and false. True if we consider that, starting with Sumer, we can follow each step taken by mankind throughout the new triad—the ages of Taurus, Aries and Pisces. False if we disregard the antediluvian kingdoms . . .

However that may be, after 6,000 years of absence or slow recuperation, we find that human beings have suddenly returned (or reappeared?) at Sumer in Mesopotamia, in China, Egypt and America. How can one fail to be astonished by the sudden emergence of these organised civilisations? All at once, so it seems, we see the Sumerians 'discover' (rediscover?) irrigation, which Plato described as an Atlantean invention, as well as pottery, polychromy, the smelting and use of metals such as copper, bronze, silver and gold . . . Sumer also yielded the first known examples of writing, engraved on clay tablets.

The sudden flowering of such an advanced civilisation inevitably raises questions. One could say the same about ancient Egypt. There we have a population of nomadic shepherds who settled in the valley of the Nile. And almost instantaneously a brilliant civilisation rises from the void, a civilisation that has no point of reference, but demonstrates an artistic refinement that we still envy. Some of the pieces from the treasure of Tutankhamun can boast of a goldsmith's technique that we would find hard to imitate. How could such a rich civilisation arise so quickly, out of nothing?

In the absence of any proto-history, one can hardly help thinking of some contribution from outside. The theory of a renaissance of Atlantean knowledge in both Egypt and Sumer automatically springs to mind. Such knowledge could have been brought about by the migratory wave of survivors of the Flood, who gradually blended with the more primitive local populations. The historian Diodorus Siculus wrote: 'The Egyptians were foreigners who, in the distant past, settled on the banks of the Nile, bringing with them the civilisation of their mother-land, the art of writing and a developed language. They came from the direction of the setting sun and they were the most ancient of men.'

It is also possible that the Atlanteans, insatiable colonisers and great voyagers, had left repositories containing the sum of their knowledge in the area around the Nile and the Euphrates. Today modern humanity is sending special capsules far out into space. They contain informative tapes on which the whole of mankind's achievements are compressed. Why not imagine that the Atlanteans before us did something similar, so that a civilisation influenced by their discoveries could get off to a good start?

The statue of the Sphinx might well have been the receptacle of their Tradition. We know that its origin and the date of its construction are still a contro-versial topic. Some scholars go so far as to claim that this colossal statue, so consistent with Atlantean achievements, was built *before* the Flood. In that case the traces of erosion that can clearly be seen below the Sphinx's head would mark the highest level reached by the flood waters. May not this inde-structible and inscrutable animal have sheltered within itself the knowledge acquired by Atlantean science?

In this way the inhabitants of the Nile Valley could have had access to an extremely profound knowledge that gave birth to a culture teeming with symbols and capable of expressing itself in an encoded language. The mysterious caste of Egyptian priests and scholars, those great initiates, appeared at the same time. Initiated into what, if not the Atlantean Knowledge? Did not the Egyptians go to the length of conferring divine powers on the great architect Imhotep, minister of the Pharaoh Zoser? Today we know that the pyramids of Gizeh are not simple Pharaonic tombs, but veritable 'books in stone'. Their positions, the relations between their measurements, are irrefutable evidence of the Egyptians' amazing astronomical and mathematical knowledge. The Sumerians, for their part, were already using the number zero, which enabled them to make cosmic calculations . . . As for the Babylonian astronomers, they knew of the existence of the great precessional year which they had calculated with remarkable accuracy.

These ancient civilisations also knew of the existence of constellations invisible to the naked eye, which were not 'discovered' until the seventeenth century, or even the nineteenth, with the help of the telescope! Where did they acquire this knowledge? Was it not the legacy of the Red Men and, going farther back, of the Elohim?

Through the intermediation of Moses, the Hebraic and then the Christian cultures benefited from this Atlantean heritage. Found among the bulrushes on the banks of the Nile, the infant Moses was taken up by the Pharaoh's daughter and 'was learned in all the wisdom of the Egyptians', so the Acts of the Apostles tell us.

The extraordinary wealth of scholars of all kinds in ancient Greece may also have its source on the banks of the Nile. Thales of Miletus studied under the Egyptian priests, then returned to his own country to teach (long before Copernicus and Kepler) that the earth was round, something already known to the Mesopotamians. Pythagoras, too, brought back his knowledge of numbers and astral movements from Egypt.

Such examples could be multiplied *ad infinitum.* May I just remind you that the sage Solon was another who made his educational pilgrimage to Egypt. It was there that he heard the story of Atlantis. When he expressed amazement at the sources of his teachers' knowledge, they replied: 'All that was written down long ago, here in our temples, and saved from oblivion . . .'

*   *   *

In conclusion I should like to tell you about a personal experience which readers of my earlier book will probably find easier to accept than others. They already know the nature of the links that unite me with the Earth. When I travel abroad, I receive positive or negative vibrations, as if the ground wished to welcome me or warn me. There are countries where I feel I am 'returning' to a land which was once, in a previous life, my native land. So you can imagine the sensations of familiarity I felt during a stay in Egypt. Old memories, at first of simple images, then of faithful reconstructions, have convinced me that I once lived in the Valley of the Kings.

I made my first 'actual' journey to Egypt some time after the Six-Day War. President Nasser was still on bad terms with France, which had supported Israel, but there was talk of a reconciliation. To mark the return to normal relations someone had had the idea of organising a fashion parade at the foot of the Pyramids. But to avoid ruffling susceptibilities, the organisers did not want a couturier who was too typically French. So the choice went to a couturier with a difference: Paco Rabanne. That was how I had the chance to seal the resumption of Franco-Egyptian understanding by presenting my latest collection in front of the Sphinx at Gizeh.

After the parade, moved by the exceptional beauty of the site which was accentuated by the unreal light of the moon, I climbed alone up the small slope which runs the length of the Sphinx's left paw. My gaze was turned to the impressive silhouette of the pyramid of Cheops, and I dreamt of the secrets it contained in its labyrinths. Suddenly, moved by a kind of inner summons, I turned back towards the Sphinx, whose sombre profile was outlined against the moon.

I was petrified. The statue appeared to me as a holographic image—in other words, the black mass of stone was outlined by a translucent veil which formed the exact shape of its original contour. What I was seeing was the Sphinx intact, just as it looked at the time of its construction. To my amazement I found that the statue was coloured. The face was painted red; the head covering blue and white.

Then I heard the Sphinx speaking to me. He explained that he was the symbol of alchemic work intended to purify his animal condition so that he could attain the divine. The Sphinx has the body of a lion; he is stretched out on the ground as if anchored to earthly matter, but his face is human. His gaze is turned towards an admittedly mysterious truth, although one can see that it brings him absolute serenity. Contemplating the sun, he himself becomes a god.

While I was slowly soaking in these revelations, I thought I saw the stone gradually lose its opacity. An open stairway appeared in the right-hand paw of the Sphinx. It led to a cavity in which all the secrets of Atlantis were hidden away. This chamber contained the definitive proof that an antediluvian civilisation which knew how to write, but also possessed complicated machines and a highly developed science, had once existed on Earth.

But soon the stone became opaque again, the secret room and the stairway disappeared. 'When my

face is restored, these treasures will be discovered,'
the Sphinx whispered to me.

Today restoration work on the face is under way.
And I learnt recently that the right paw of the gigantic statue is covered in a forest of scaffolding. Access
to it is forbidden to the public. Does this mean that
excavations underneath the paw have begun?

Soon this Atlantean knowledge, which was the
source of one of the greatest human civilisations,
but which, manipulated for evil ends by the Sons of
Belial, also caused its downfall, may possibly see the
light of day again. Is this because it needs to be
revealed to certain chosen ones so that it may be
passed on? Like the sons of Belial, modern mankind
has known for some decades how to use atomic
energy to change the earth's axis. This is no more
than a theory, but if it is put into practice, enormous
cataclysms can be foreseen and then it will be the
turn of the survivors of this 'end of the world' to find a
new hiding-place for the secret Atlantean knowledge
which would no longer be safe in Egypt.

*

The site of the Sphinx and the pyramids was, in fact,
chosen for its extraordinary stability. These monuments must have been in a geological sector completely protected from any seismic activity. So the
secret of the Atlanteans was well guarded.

Nevertheless, an event that I found very alarming
happened in 1992. For the first time an earthquake
had the pyramid of Cheops as its epicentre. I hope
that that need not be seen as a sign of very ill omen.

Following the Sons of Belial, have we gone too far
in the misuse of our innovative intelligence? Have we
distanced ourselves from the divine to the point that
he comes to recall us to order in this place where
human knowledge is safe?

Everything suggests that human beings, having

reached a certain stage of evolution, are inevitably condemned to destruction in the form of a flood or some other cataclysm. Does this mean that the Gods are jealous of the ascent of Man?

Chapter 4

KNOWLEDGE MISUSED

Science without conscience can only be the ruin of the soul.

Rabelais

The ancient Egyptians, as guardians of the Knowledge, wisely reserved access to it to a selected few. Was it because they had already calculated the risks of its being wrongly exploited? Since then, and down the millennia, the initiates have often been forced to adopt a protective cloak of occultism. They did so to prevent the diffusion of a knowledge which they foresaw could lead to the most terrible disasters if it got into the wrong hands. So the light was put under a bushel. The Gospel according to St Matthew (7:6) warns us: '. . . neither cast ye your pearls before swine, lest they trample them under their feet, and turn again and rend you.'

Unfortunately the evolution of our contemporary world seems to confirm all their anxieties. Because it has become the instrument of a frigid technocracy, human intelligence shoulders a heavy responsibility in this age of perpetual crisis. Hasn't it, for example, been used far too often for the purpose of massive destruction? Names such as Hiroshima and Chernobyl have seriously discredited science's image. Will it ever recover? Today, the public still looks on it with some suspicion, because of the terrible damage caused.

Nevertheless, it seems to me futile to attack the

scientists in that way. I doubt if they have ever deliberately worked for the destruction of mankind in the
secrecy of their libraries or laboratories. But have
they always calculated the diabolical use to which
their inventions could be put? They were happy just
to extend their understanding of the laws of the universe and pass on their discoveries. But the heirs of
these discoveries often thought up perverted ways in
which to use them. And faced with the catastrophes
that followed (or still threaten to follow), there has
sometimes been a tendency to denounce science
itself, and not the way it has been diverted from its
original intentions. When 'progress' is criticised
wholesale in this way, it is not the actual progress
that is at fault, but an 'anti-progress' inherent in
this misuse of knowledge.

*

This misconception is not new. Since the dawn of
civilisation, people have had the idea that the Gods
or the single God, driven by a jealous will to power,
tended to fight shy of their desire for knowledge.
Many myths reflect this belief, describing how the
Divinities shrank from handing over the keys of
Knowledge to humans for fear that they would come
to rival them.

I find it very hard to believe that the Creator could
be so petty, but there are plenty of examples to support this ultra-romantic thesis. It claims that mankind never received the Knowledge as a gift from
Heaven, but was forced to seize it by theft and trick-
ery, with a correspondingly terrible punishment.

Isn't that what the Sumerian legend tells us? Enki,
the god of wisdom, obstinately refused to hand over
to mankind the secrets necessary for the development of civilisation. But the goddess of Heaven,
Inanna, sided with the humans. She was heart-
broken to see them crouching in their primitive

marshes. So she visited the god Enki, who offered her a sumptuous banquet in homage to her beauty. Charmed by his guest, the host imbibed copiously. Once under the influence, he soon imparted the divine secrets to Inanna. When he came to his senses and realised that he had been duped, Enki moved heaven and earth to stop Inanna from achieving her ends. But the goddess escaped from all his traps and revealed to men the mysteries of the technique for founding a civilisation. The first impetus had been given, but not before the vigilance of the god of wisdom had been eluded.

And did not Prometheus have to commit a serious theft in order to bring fire to men? It is no longer very clear whether he sought it on the wheel of the sun or in the forges of Hephaestus, but one thing is certain: he accomplished the act without the authorisation of the Gods, who reserved the use of fire entirely for themselves.

When Zeus discovered this perfidy, he had no mercy on Prometheus, who was chained to a rock and condemned for all eternity to have his liver consumed by an eagle! The lesson seemed clear . . .

It reappears in the Christian tradition, with Lucifer playing the Promethean role. His name, which has such a bad reputation today, actually means 'light-bringer' (as opposed to Mephistopheles, 'light-hater'). Originally Lucifer was an angel completely devoted to God. Nevertheless, out of love of Creation, and perhaps out of pride, he carried the torch of knowledge to a humanity still sunk in the darkest ignorance. Lucifer was severely punished, for God made him one of the fallen angels, thrown down among the satanic forces . . .

*

A first reading of these myths and texts certainly leads us to see a revolt of men against their Creators as a factor in the flowering of civilisations and science. But I believe that things are more complicated than that. What all the tales point out is not so much the desire of humans for Knowledge (legitimate, after all) as their vaunted (and dangerous) ambition to take themselves for Gods. Did not the vanished civilisations owe their destruction to this intoxication with omnipotence?

For once mankind was armed with Knowledge and had thoroughly explored all its aspects, including the most dangerous ones, his pride knew no bounds and he persuaded himself that he could dominate the world on his own. Myth or reality, the annihilation of Atlantis dramatically illustrates this fatal process. Forgetting and denying their dependence on the divine, the Sons of Belial sought to master the planet and use it for their own ends. In so doing, they left themselves open to a terrible counter-blow from the Heavens.

True, not all the 'lost' civilisations were lost because a continent was swallowed up. But did not all of them sin out of vanity or lust, because of the gradual loss of their link with the divine? That was the case with Rome, which foundered in a sea of moral and political corruption after having dominated the Mediterranean world. The great colonial empires, whether they were Portuguese, French or British, were also victims of their own arrogance and inordinate greed. They all thought they saw the proof of their superiority in what was only a temporary hegemony. These powers had got it into their heads that the world belonged to them and that they could appropriate it at will. This presumption was to lead to their inevitable and brutal decline, although some lasted longer than others.

Brutal the fall of the Soviet empire undoubtedly was—as if to give us a sharp reminder that our errors are punished much faster in these straitened times. The Soviet Union, that vast fortress that was thought impossible to breach, suddenly disintegrated before our eyes. Surely that is the best example of a civilisation being progressively perverted? Based on an admirable principle (the equality of men), communism led to the most preposterous type of dictatorship and the most heretical of systems.

*

Humans are not the victims of advances in their knowledge, but of the vanity with which they use them. That is what another celebrated myth, the Tower of Babel, suggests to us. The people had taken it into their heads to build a tower high enough to reach up to Heaven. God was angered by this plan and reduced their efforts to nothing. It is easy to understand that the myth is not blaming the humans for their skill in assembling bricks and bitumen to build a tower! The fault of the builders of Babel was to have taken it upon themselves to dominate the Earth and force the Gate of Heaven. 'Let us make us a name!' they clamoured with overweening conceit. By trying to assert themselves, they forgot their submission to the divine power, the need to respect an ethic, even as a most elementary precaution.

Science and technology should have been no more than the means for humans to adapt themselves to the world, but they tried to turn them into instruments of conquest. Nothing wrong in rising up towards Heaven—on the contrary, that is the point of our life—always provided that this ascent is regarded not as a challenge, but as a desire for fusion with the All . . .

*   *   *

The apple eaten by Adam and Eve has often been interpreted by some biblical scholars as the symbol of Knowledge. The forbidden fruit is supposed to have caused their fall. Personally, I have always mistrusted the confusion a certain Church has managed to maintain between normal human curiosity and the satanic pride of a creature trying to exceed its limits. All the more so because this original sin was attributed (as if by chance) to the woman, because Eve was the first to bite the apple. As far as I am concerned, I do not believe for a single moment that God intended to keep mankind in ignorance. What kind of a test would it be to offer Adam and Eve the fruit of knowledge and hope that they would leave it untouched? It's ridiculous.

In my opinion, the apple probably represented man's baser instincts, those vile desires that draw him towards the material, not the spiritual world. Undoubtedly the first two created beings were warned of the dangers they might incur if they gave 'evil' a good bite. And doubtless the free will we possess today already existed in the earthly paradise. Adam and Eve did not resist. Consequently, in the same way, man will be confronted before each of his actions with the need to choose between the two different ways that are constantly offered to him: on the one hand the good that satisfies, and on the other the perilous gluttony of evil. It will be the same thing with science, which he can always tip in favour of one side or the other, for better . . . or for worse.

In the Promethean legend, for example, fire is an ambiguous symbol. It may represent heat that has been tamed, but it can also become murderous lightning. As Jacob Boehme wrote in his *Mysterium Magnum*: 'Fire is painful, whereas light is kindly, sweet and fecund.'

This shows that myths do not condemn Knowledge and human intelligence *per se*, but they warn us

against their ambiguity. Besides, the divine prohib-
itions were not so strict. Did not the gods more or
less close their eyes to the theft of fire? Was not Prometheus finally freed from his terrible fate by Hercules?
Later, after the death of the Centaur, Prometheus
even achieved immortality. Nevertheless, the punishment he suffered remains as a warning to humans
that they are responsible for the use they make of
revelations from which they will benefit . . .

*

In this field, the record of our contemporary civilisation is far from brilliant. Men have put knowledge
to wrong uses, they have forgotten its spiritual
dimension. As we reach the end of Kali Yuga, science
and especially technology have distanced themselves
from their divine source. You will recall the words of
Descartes calling on man to make himself 'master
and possessor of nature'. In so doing, he wrought a
catastrophic break between the thinking ego and the
world considered as external object, simply matter
for experiments. Nature became a vast field of action
for experimenters who worked on it to their heart's
content.

This was the point of departure for an exploitation
of the world, the results of which we have already
seen: laying waste of the environment, chemical pollution, deforestation, the greenhouse effect . . . The
record is catastrophic. Responsibility for it falls on
the division that a misdirected science once thought
it could establish between Mankind and Nature.
Today we are only beginning to understand how far
we have gone astray. What idiots we are! We have
forgotten that the universe was a whole and that we
were an essential part of it. While subjecting Nature,
we were enslaving ourselves . . .

Some peoples whom we call 'primitive' knew this
better than we did. In 1855, the Chief of the Duwar-

ish Indian tribe gave this moving speech before the American President, as his fellow Indians were preparing to go to the tiny reserve allocated to them:

> Every part of this land is sacred to my people, every pine needle, every sandy beach, every cloud in the dark forests. We are part of the land and it is a part of us. The fragrant flowers are our sisters, the squirrel, the horse, the great eagle, are our brothers. The Earth is our mother. Whoever attacks her attacks the sons of the earth as well. When people spit on the earth, they spit on themselves. For the earth, we know, does not belong to man, man belongs to the earth, which the red man loves like a newborn babe loves the beating of its mother's heart.

*   *   *

But far be it from me to draw the reader into a blanket denigration of science. We all know how much we have owed, for centuries, to scientific progress, in our everyday comfort, our struggle against suffering and our understanding of the world. And when we fall ill, we all behave like Socrates: we prefer to summon the doctor rather than the philosopher, 'the second in all things'.

Nevertheless, I am worried . . . And you would be entitled to ask if I am an old fogey, if I am not making a terrible fuss about a few scientific discoveries that are probably nothing to be scared of. I am suddenly afraid of sounding like some nineteenth-century grousers who were fiercely opposed to the railways under ridiculous pretexts: the infernal speed of the trains would stun the passengers who, exposed to the wind, would also swallow all the unwholesome exhalations of the earth, if they did not catch pneumonia from going through the tunnels . . . I imagine that on the day when some handyman invented the wheel, there was an old fool nearby to predict that the end of mankind was nigh. Then why not continue to have faith in progress!

One could counter that with the ecological disasters we have already mentioned. But that would not be enough. If I worry about the possible misuses of science, it is because it is on the brink of an unprecedented breakthrough. Until now, technical progress has remained in the field of *innovation*. The invention of the tool multiplied man's strength by ten, but it was still only a mechanical extension of his arm. What we are now seeing is a veritable *mutation*, symptomatic of the passage from one zodiacal era to another. Tools are no longer simply our docile servants, they are on the way to surpassing us. The computer is no longer content to calculate faster than the human brain, it makes calculations beyond man's capacity. Soon, biochemical molecules will be substituted for the silicon and gallium of electronic components; their capacity for storing information will then come close to that of the living cell. We are on the eve of what the specialists call the fourth generation of robots—that is to say 'intelligent' machines, capable of capturing the data from their environment and acting in consequence.

Are we in a position to envisage all the repercussions of such a mutation? If mankind becomes a virtual demiurge, a subordinate being, shall we not be the victims of our own creations? At all events, faced with the unheard-of potentialities of research, we need now more than ever to assure ourselves that scientists place their discipline under the control of a proper ethic or, more simply, of a sense of responsibility.

It is all a question of balance and proportion. That seemed to be the message of the great savant Daedalus to his son Icarus when he was preparing to fly with wings fixed to his shoulders with wax. 'Do not fly too low,' his inventor father told him, 'or your wings will not support you. Do not fly too high, or the heat of the sun will melt the wax.' But Icarus, intoxicated by the altitude, rose higher and higher, as if to join the gods. The sun melted the wax and the vainglorious boy plunged into the sea.

At the point we have now reached, it is not indulging in simplistic antirationalism to say that modern science, likewise, has the means to lead us into the abyss. It is up to all of us to be vigilant . . . always supposing that that may be enough . . .

*

Has anyone heard of Goiania? Hardly anybody. Yet a few years ago this town in Brazil was the scene of a news item or rather a drama which may seem to us like a kind of parable about the dangers of Promethean fire. In an abandoned medical laboratory a scrap-merchant recovered a machine used in the treatment of cancer. While dismantling it, he found a large lead cylinder which he opened by beating it with a hammer. The cylinder contained a pretty bluish, slightly phosphorescent powder. He gave some of it to his children and then to fascinated neighbours.

The powder was caesium 137, an extremely radioactive element. The scrap-merchant's wife and children died a few days later. Others were exposed to enormous radiation levels which condemned them to an early death. Hundreds of people were affected and many families had to be evacuated from their houses, which had to be razed to the ground. Such mayhem caused by radioactivity has never been seen before outside the former USSR.

Here we have an apparatus whose function was to cure a disease and which nevertheless became responsible for the destruction of a community . . .

Can one think of a better example of the ever-possible mishandling of technology?

Of course, in this case it was only simple human error, a gratuitous misuse. The most dangerous threat is the deliberate and permanent misuse of science for murderous ends.

Atomic fission *per se* is not evil. Properly controlled and with the tricky problem of waste disposal solved, it could provide a genuine solution to our energy problems. But in the meantime, the misapplication of nuclear research has forced us to run tremendous risks for nearly half a century. A formidable sword of Damocles hangs over our heads. The full complement of nuclear armament today is calculated by specialists to be the equivalent of fifteen billion tons of TNT! A figure too enormous for the mind to take in. It works out at three tons of explosive per inhabitant of the planet! When the scientists, in an attempt to warn us, tell us that we are sitting on a barrel of gunpowder, it is not a metaphor, but a physical reality! One day, when arms are distributed to a whole population on some trifling pretext, it is bound to explode into wholesale slaughter.

Strategists have long taken shelter behind the concept of the 'deterrent' to explain the mad arms race we have witnessed during recent decades. To guarantee its safety, a country had to be able to persuade its enemies that it could reply to a nuclear attack. Today this 'deterrent' is nothing but a con. If a massive nuclear attack took place, we know that not only the country attacked would be destroyed, but the whole biosphere . . . even if the recipient had no time to reply. A war or even a chain of accidents would leave only losers behind.

Finally convinced of the inanity of their warlike folly, the great powers have launched a campaign to reduce their nuclear armament. An encouraging sign, certainly, but more than enough remains to send the planet into another orbit . . .

Because they set the pace in innovation, scientists are able to forecast our prospects and their pronouncements sometimes sound like prophecies. Let us hope, however, that the great chemist Marcelin Bethelot was wrong when he wrote at the end of the nineteenth century:

> I foresee that after some hundred years of physical and chemical science, man will know what the atom is . . . And I believe that when man has reached this point, God will descend on Earth with his enormous bunch of keys and say to mankind: 'Gentlemen, it is the end of Time!'

*   *   *

Today the dangers inherent in matters nuclear are comparatively well-known, although it took some terrible accidents to open our eyes. But another, subtler, threat is appearing. Although it is still in its infancy the science of genetics is enough to send a shudder down one's spine, especially if one thinks of the ways in which it could be exploited.

You will remember the commotion caused by the sudden 'resignation' of one of the world's foremost specialists in this field. He had succeeded in freezing embryos, which in itself could be regarded as an extraordinary scientific feat, and even a hope for humanity. However, this geneticist preferred a kind of professional suicide to pursuing research with potential future repercussions that petrified him. He was nonetheless aware that, even if it helped to alert public opinion, his personal decision would not be enough to halt the irresistible march of genetics. His colleagues continue with their researches, unprotected by guidelines and controlled by unscrupulous financial interests. What sort of a world are they preparing for us in their test-tubes? Even if it does not disappear, mankind might well lose the familiar face we know, which is equally frightening . . .

*

Nature has performed the miracle of never producing two exactly identical beings (except in the special case of twins coming from a single egg). Yet this infinite diversity is only the variation of a unique and eternal molecule, deoxyribonucleic acid, better known as DNA.

This molecule appears in the form of a double helix, in the image of the kundalini, the vital force which, according to the Hindus, coils round our spinal column. Recalling the original movement that was the basis of all creation, this double helix, beneath its apparent mobility, symbolises simultaneously the fecundity and the permanence of being. Because it is susceptible of an infinite number of combinations, the DNA molecule is the creative source of all human beings, as well as the symbol of a permanence: that of our humanity.

This molecule, present in each of the some five billion cells to be found in a male adult's body, was only discovered about 40 years ago. Today we are able to choose from its sequences, modify them and stick them together again. We shall soon be in a position to make those clones that have long been favourites with science fiction which, as we know to our cost, is often prophetic. It will be possible to make a biological double of absolutely any human being. It will 'suffice' to remove the genetic inheritance contained in the nucleus of any single cell in order to insert it into an ovum. The child born as the result of this manipulation will be the exact twin of the donor of the DNA.

Such a scientific 'breakthrough' can be exploited for better or for worse. What a glorious prospect for the food industry, which will be able to select the most productive animals and make a spectacular increase in our resources! On the other hand, what a worry for mankind! Are we moving towards a society capable of deliberately fashioning the type of man it needs? Will the rich and powerful be able to order science to 'breed' their personal clones, in order to prolong their lives by removing the organs they need from these counterparts?

An apocalyptic prospect . . . Researchers, for their part, see a source of hope in genetic manipulations. Locating the site of hereditary illnesses which are registered in the DNA code is one example. But there is quite a difference between detecting a genetic anomaly and curing it. In the case of a recognised anomaly, there is a risk that the solution adopted might be the therapeutic abortion and short-term elimination of bearers of 'abnormal' genes. That leaves the door open to births by selection, a kind of social eugenics. All those not meeting the criteria demanded by society could be choked off 'in the egg'. Those whose illnesses or handicaps are going to be too heavy for the community to bear, those whose intellectual or physical potentialities are not going to meet a need, would be irremediably marginalised . . . Of course, it would all be done under the pretext of ensuring improved viability for the social group. There would be no lack of experts to justify this vast genetic screening process on financial or population grounds . . .

*

You will say that we have not reached that point yet and that I am adopting the viewpoint of a disaster scenario. The long-term consequences of biological and genetic discoveries still seem rather hazy. Yet there are good reasons for us to be on our guard. The ability to determine the sex of a foetus at an early stage may look like a minor step forward, and a quite innocent one at that. Nevertheless, in some countries this 'progress' has already caused the mass slaughter of girl children, pregnant women preferring abortion when they learnt that they would not give birth to a boy. Today clinics even offer the possibility of choosing the sex of one's child for a few thousand francs. What will the next stage be? That reminds me of a project that looked farcical in 1979. The Americans had the hairbrained idea of stocking the sperm of Nobel Prizewinners, with the ill-concealed aim of creating a race of geniuses . . .

Today people in general are opening their eyes and demanding the widespread formation of ethical committees which would be responsible for monitoring genetic advances. Such advances would have to undergo a study aiming to evaluate the positive and negative consequences of the so-called 'progress'. But the very existence of such ethical committees is a terrible admission. If they have proved necessary, it is because science seems to have lost all ability to tell good from bad. I shall be told that that was never its role. Well, I say the opposite! Ancient science, based on the secret Knowledge, never forgot that it was there to serve a purpose: coming closer to the divine, not descent into hell. Modern science has lost what the Tradition knew, what the Egyptians were able to preserve. For too long it has abandoned any concept of morality by claiming that this does not come within its domain. Today we can see the slippery slope and the confusion to which this disclaiming attitude has led us! Undoubtedly there is hope in the fact that the scientists themselves have now pressed the alarm button, but will their warnings be heeded?

Or must we await the fatal moment foretold by Isaiah (2:11) when 'The lofty looks of man shall be humbled, and the haughtiness of men shall be bowed down, and the Lord alone shall be exalted in that day.'

* * *

But I do not want my remarks to be misunderstood. Once again, my diatribe is directed not so much against science itself as against its misuse. Indeed, what I *am* opposed to is scientism, the attempt to reduce the human being to a few mathematical propositions. The modern age has stopped asking itself about the *why* of the world to concentrate solely on the *how*. It is forgetting the origin and meaning of life and concerning itself only with life's mechanical functioning. I fear that a society deprived of any spiritual principle is doomed to break up, like the builders of the Tower of Babel.

Having said that, if one is entitled to point an accusing finger at science, it is only because it has moved away from its original goals. If it finds the right path again, it will form our best chance for survival. To make things quite clear: if I had to choose between science and taking refuge in bogus irrationalism, I should choose science without hesitation! I know full well that there will be no satisfactory solution to the difficulties confronting us without the support of scientific research. It is scientific research that can teach us to ration our resources by developing substitute energy, that can tackle epidemics and, lastly, that will be able to feed a growing population. Biotechnology should be able to facilitate the low-cost mass-production of edible proteins based on substrata such as natural gas or agricultural waste. Of course, gourmets will be scandalised, but we shall be husbanding our land and above all saving millions of human lives.

What I am really appealing for is not the end of the reign of science, but its subjection to mankind's well-being. What I am hoping is that awareness of their responsibilities by all scientists will accompany the formidable period of change that is under way. We all know Einstein's celebrated remark which is unfortunately still as apposite as ever: 'The power unleashed by the atom has changed everything, except our way of thinking, and we are sliding towards an unprecedented disaster: a new way of thinking is essential if we are to survive.'

* * *

I am not sure that I can hear this new way of thinking vibrate clearly in the concert of voices raised today against the abuses of technology. The protestations of a certain number of ecologists in particular seem to me to have strange ultra-conservative echoes.

If people who drive Morris Minors tend to make me laugh, those who choose candles to light their houses make me furious. Ecology should not be synonymous with return to the age of Cro-Magnon man. The age of Aquarius should facilitate a forward, not a backward leap. Unfortunately, I find too many 'nature' lovers are people who have simply reinforced their hate of modernism by using nature as a loophole. The genuine ecologists do not have an archaic attitude.

An attitude to which I obviously cannot subscribe. All my life, I have made a point of keeping in step with modernity. So much so that I have sometimes been called an avant-gardist, a deviation that I finally took as an insult. On the contrary, I am firmly anchored in the present and that is what I demonstrate in my fashion collections. I am not ahead of my time. It is those who call me avant-gardist who are missing the boat . . .

I am in agreement with the ecologists on a number of points. I share their analysis about the urgent need for global action to save our environment and even our planet. But I distrust those who hide beneath their profession of faith the sterile nostalgia for a grandpa's world which holds no particular attraction for me. Why should we throw out wholesale the improvements in our comfort and our well-being? Night-time by a wood fire may have been picturesque, but electricity and central heating have their good side, too. Laundresses, gleaners and ironing women undoubtedly made fine subjects for paintings, but I prefer to think that these women would have found their work less backbreaking with the help of mechanical inventions.

In my opinion, a certain number of ecological 'fundamentalists' have an irritating tendency to seek their ideal society in the past rather than in the future. I have even heard sociobiologists dreaming aloud of a world in which mankind would have succeeded in imitating 'the nuclear family of the white-handed gibbon or the harmonious community of the bees'. True, we are descendants from the animal kingdom. I explained elsewhere that our first incarnations may have been as animals. But the direction of evolution is always and inevitably upwards. So no misplaced nostalgia, for heaven's sake; we rise, we do not descend!

I should not be very surprised to hear certain extremists telling us that AIDS forms part of the autoregulatory mechanisms of Gaia, or that eugenics is the only answer to population growth. We shall return to the false prophets later on. In the meantime, let us always be suspicious of those in whom passion for nature barely conceals an aversion for humanity.

*   *   *

Aversion and hate . . . Perhaps that is where the greatest fault committed by our civilisation lies. We have forgotten that God is not only Knowledge, but Love as well. We have forgotten that human intelligence is no more than a cold monster, unless it is guided and supported by an ardent spirituality.

And the Apocalypse will come from this lack of Love. For too long now we have been operating under the rule of a 'science without conscience'. If we are shamelessly making holes in the ozone layer, isn't it because we take no interest in the fate of our children? Isn't it out of lack of brotherly feeling that we use poor countries as our dustbin? Isn't it out of total inhumanity that we are killing children in South America to swell the 'donations of organs' which in themselves could be justified if they were not the object of trafficking and crime.

Born of the secret Knowledge, science has progressively turned itself into a great harlot. It has sold itself to market forces, it has become the slave of financial interests. It has fostered in the public the creation of false needs which have led to our society of excess and wastage. By leading itself astray, the Knowledge has made us lose all notion of the sacred. Today, everything has become merchandise: blood, organs, even sperm.

In such a climate, it would be useless to make science in itself the scapegoat for all our ills. It is only an instrument of our evil designs. Perhaps it was responsible for Hiroshima and Chernobyl. But no advanced technology was necessary to build the gas chambers and crematoria at Auschwitz.

If our planet Gaia now suffers from chemical pollution, strangulation by concrete and a general deterioration of the environment, it is also being slowly asphyxiated by the blackness of our thoughts, which sooner or later will end by provoking the wrath of the *earth*, as well as the Heavens.

Chapter 5

WHEN THE BLUE PLANET WEARS BLACK

*Come, my children, awake from this
sleep, for the world may be cast down at
any moment.*

Message from the Virgin at
San Damiano, 1967.

My career as a couturier very soon gave me plenty of
opportunities to travel abroad. From the '60s
onwards I was able to travel to the four continents
to present my fashion collections. Insatiably curious
about all cultures and all kinds of scenery, I explored
the world with the sensual pleasure of a Baudelaire
dreaming of a young giantess whose 'magnificent
forms' he could 'traverse at leisure'.

I was not the only one to be intoxicated by the
splendours and the 'powerful verve' of Nature. For
the first time in the history of mankind, a generation
of men and women discovered with amazement the
extraordinary beauty of their Blue Planet, thanks to
the photographs taken by the astronauts.

Unfortunately, my recent travels (from Russia to
Brazil, from Canada to Japan) have made an entirely
different impression. The face the Earth offers today
is of quite another sort. Everywhere I felt a grey uni-
formity swiftly gaining ground. Seen from the sky,
the towns of the whole world seemed to be covered
with a layer of filth, when they had not actually disappeared under the rubbish.

During one of the last missions by the American
space-ship, an astronaut also noted the changes our

poor planet had undergone. In some places, gases emitted by our industries were making the atmosphere opaque to infra-red thermic radiation. By observing the Earth from space, it was seen that their spectral 'signatures' were spreading far and wide.

But I am not convinced that chemical pollution alone is responsible. The blackness I observed, as I see it, is also the darkness that transpires from our dismal, rancorous or even downright evil souls. Every time a thought runs through our minds, we emit a vibration known as a 'Watcher'. When they are negative, these 'Watchers' pollute our mental space and that of our surroundings. We know how a 'bad mood' can be catching. Go into the room or office of someone who is in a 'black humour' (such expressions are never fortuitous) and you will feel a weight descend on your shoulders. Added together on the scale of a town or a country, these negative waves form a covering that weighs on our psyche in an almost palpable fashion and fosters in its turn hate, jealousy and bitterness.

About two years ago, when I was walking peacefully down a street in Paris, I suddenly felt as if I was imprisoned by darkness thicker and more viscous than liquid tar. The passers-by had disappeared, there was nothing but black dirt all round me. When this terrifying shroud brushed against my body, I screamed. The obscurity vanished immediately. I found myself in the light of the street again and people staring at me in astonishment!

The whole business only lasted a few seconds, I suppose. But when I came to myself, I reread the passages about the Three Days of the Lord. And I understood that I had just had the visionary experience of the terrible darkness that will reign over the Blue Planet when the divine wrath falls upon it.

Since then, I have continued to watch this heartrending veil which is tarnishing the colours of the world. 'This dark age will go on darkening itself until its end,' the *Vishnu Purana* says. Everything on Earth is striving to climb towards the clarity of the Fourth Vibratory Plane and we are weighing ourselves down, we are sinking into the opaqueness of matter. Some kind of tearing apart is inevitable.

*   *   *

Already twilight is descending on this age of Pisces, condemned by the cycle of time. But if this transition from one age to another is unavoidable, it will only entail our destruction to the extent that we contribute to it. The clouds that gather over our destiny are only the result of our own darkness.

The chief culprit is egoism, the negative feeling that eats into our minds. To put it in a better light, we often call it by the more flattering name of individualism. But it is responsible for putting the blinkers on our thoughts and lowering our inner vibrations.

If Prometheus was the symbol of the conquests in the dawn of Time, Narcissus is surely the symbol of the end of Kali Yuga. Not content with forgetting the divine, we have abandoned the public sphere to concentrate on ourselves alone. Without a shadow of doubt, the predominant religion is the cult of the I. Excessive body-building, implants to restore virility, and endless face-lifts: *mens sana in corpore sano?* There has been a great change in our mentalities: we are more interested in appearances than *being*. No one wants to age, no one wants to die, or hand down their experiences, or share anything at all. Social success alone is no longer the expected reward for a job well done, there must also be an increase in power, in material possessions, in displays of wealth. And please leave me alone, my conscience! The least tremor in their souls makes the worshippers of the

Ego rush to their 'shrink', who will offer them a flattering mirror: talk to me about me, that's all I'm interested in. We want to be comfortable here and now, and every man for himself.

And what about the Earth in all this egoism? The Earth and its inhabitants (the others), the future of the world, of our world, meaning our future? No one, or hardly anyone, takes it seriously! That attitude however, is what will ruin us collectively, and therefore individually. Every profound egoist finds himself in the ridiculous position of a man decorating the interior of his house down to the last detail, without realising that a landslide outside is threatening to swallow it up. Indeed, how could the human beings of today notice the state of the world surrounding them, when they are permanently occupied with following the ups and downs of their superficial I? Oh yes, they have heard about the ecological disasters, and the racial conflicts that ravage the planet, they even follow the developments in the press, but their interest never exceeds the stage of fleeting astonishment, between the entertainment section and the sports pages. If need be, they shed a tear over so many mishaps, or pick out something to talk about at a society dinner, just to show that they are up to date. To be well informed: that is a programme made to measure for these frivolous types; but to get involved, put one's hand in one's pocket or militate, that is another matter. Above all do not disturb: I am asleep.

Today this universal self-centredness is the biggest obstacle to the planetary mobilisation called for by both scientists and initiates. In any case, how can one make oneself heard by people who walk the streets with a Walkman on their ears or shut themselves up at home in a comfortable cocoon? 'Communicate', you say? But are not all the innovations of modern life (from automatic vendors to teletext) aimed at reducing our contacts with other people to a minimum? Others? There is no harm in tolerating them, provided they stay in their little corner and keep their distance. Otherwise, one will defend one's national, ethnic or religious territory. The hour of closed ranks and criminal purging has struck. Does it, even now, signal the start of the great war of the end of Time?

*

Some people will undoubtedly think that, in the majority of 'democratic' countries, we have not reached that stage and that, far from it, we claim to be benefactors of the poor and defenders of human rights on the rest of the planet. A kind of 'paying our dues' by a few localised interventions. But what example are we setting, we the lesson givers? The only order our civilisation now obeys is—material comfort! And personal comfort at that . . . For it has nothing to do with an ideal of general well-being, but with a personal plethora that we dare to call happiness. I cannot remember who said that the quest for an individual happiness that does not aim to spread it around among others is no more than a 'predator's dream'. Thus we pursue our goals without worrying about those we shall have to trample on as we go.

'He who possesses much money will be the master of men,' says the *Vishnu Purana*, evoking the end of this Kali Yuga that announces the great disaster:

Amassing a fortune will be the most widely shared objective. The mind of men will be essentially occupied with the search for material gratifications and power. Spiritual values will decline from day to day, the world will become depraved. Ownership and fortune alone will confer rank:

physical health will be the sole source of devotion, and the passions will be sexual. Lies and falsehoods will be the means of success.

Drawn to the slope of easy pleasure by the cult of the ego, our civilisation is sliding slowly towards moral corruption. A certain morality involving effort and search has been replaced by the hedonistic principle of 'everything, now'. Drugs, sex and gambling invade the planet, adding daily burdens to mankind's karma, and that blackness that no bank will ever be able to 'launder'. Hate rages in the pop songs, violence even invades the games meant for children, love is losing its chances of survival. Jeremiah adjures us: 'Return ye now everyone from his evil way and from the evil of your doing.' But who remembers Jeremiah now? Instead of his imprecations, we prefer the alluring calls of the adman: expensive cars for glamour boys, deluxe meals against a background of secret rendezvous, eroticism in the service of washing-up powders. 'Egoist, egoist!' cry the women, revolted yet seduced, in an opera setting. 'Become diabolical!', advises a superb woman made up as a she-devil in order to sell a brand of stockings.

Of course, a place must be found for humour in all this marketing. But this kind of humour does not look innocent to me, insofar as it reflects our deep-seated inclinations. We are already diabolical. We shall become even more so, if we do not change our way of thinking. And so we shall roll out the red carpet for the Antichrist, the emanation proclaimed by Satan. When he appears, it will be too late for regrets. 'You summoned me,' he will say, 'here I am . . .'

*   *   *

All this imaginative depiction of ill-distributed luxuries as perverted pleasures reminds me irresistibly of the 'great whore' of the Revelation of St John, who 'was arrayed in purple and scarlet colour, and decked with gold and precious stones and pearls . . . And upon her forehead was a name written, MYSTERY, BABYLON THE GREAT, THE MOTHER OF HARLOTS AND ABOMINATIONS OF THE EARTH.' That wonderful city was doomed to fall, because everything in it was based on temporal values. Wealth and power had perverted its people, extinguishing any spiritual dimension in them. But Babylon is also a symbol for the whole history of mankind. The Bible is full of allusions to other cities of the same kind destroyed by the wrath of the Lord—for example, Sodom and Gomorrah, where vice reigned. And everywhere it is said that in the time of greatest tribulations, the punishment of the 'new Babylons' will be carried out in an even more terrible fashion.

Is it by chance that a city like Los Angeles, today one of the most corrupt on the planet, capital of illusion and artifice, where the cult of the body and money dominate, where drugs and violence are completely out of control, is it by chance that this city is situated on a telluric fault which could cause its destruction in a few minutes? Edgar Cayce, the great American clairvoyant, predicted that such a catastrophe would inevitably take place before the end of the century. Geologists are well aware that this prophecy might come true and that San Francisco would be in danger, too.

Many Mediterranean towns are in danger of suffering the same fate. For have not they also become modern Babylons? Are they not guilty of terrible ecological pollution? Concrete buildings, sewers, draining oil, heavy metals . . . The Mediterranean is now recognised as one of the most polluted regional seas in the world. Yet this is the bath in which millions come to immerse themselves every year in search of . . . what? Words fail me. Moreover, to make matters worse, this part of the world is controlled by corruption on a gigantic and Mafia-like scale. Dubious real estate operations destroy the coast-line while casinos and clandestine drug laboratories are responsible for the ruin of souls. Nostradamus had already lamented the fate of this region (Tenth Century, quatrain 60):

> I weep for Nice, Monaco, Pisa, Genoa,
> Savona, Siena, Capua, Modena, Malta,
> Above, blood, and sword as a New Year's gift,
> fire, earth tremors, water, ill-starred night.

Or, in the Seventh Century, quatrain 6:

> Naples, Palermo and all Sicily
> will be depopulated by the hand of the barbarian,
> Corsica, Salerno and the Island of Sardinia,
> Starvation, plague, war, the end of evils embarked
>   upon.

So one night (*nolte*) would suffice to wipe out the Italian peninsula and the French Côte d'Azur. But many other towns would be affected. The prophecy of Prémol, which I quoted earlier, had predicted the internecine conflicts that would ruin the mercantile and cultural splendour of the Lebanese capital: 'Thou, superb Tyre (to the south of Beirut) who still escapest the storm, do not rejoice in thy pride. The eruption of the volcano which shall burn thy entrails approaches.' The same prophecy of Prémol also warns the town of Jerusalem (the ancient capital of Judea, near Palestine, now occupied by the Israelis), whose persistent intransigence was known: 'Jerusalem. Jerusalem. Save thyself from the fire of Sodom and Gomorrah and the sack of Babylon.' Zechariah (12:3) had already warned us what a danger Jerusalem would represent for the safety of the world, as the Palestinian problem and Intifada, the 'revolution of the stones', show us today: 'And in that day I will make Jerusalem a burdensome stone for all people: all that burden themselves with it shall be cut in pieces.'

And that is not all. Other metropolises seem to be threatened. In the first rank of these, most prophecies give pride of place to Paris, the 'Babylon of Gaul', and Rome, which they rechristen by the name of the 'Great Whore'. We shall have occasion to return to the subject later on . . .

* * *

Of course, we should pull ourselves together, fight against this relaxing of moral standards, this squandering of riches regardless of misery, this desire for the self-sufficiency of privileges. But how to achieve it, when the whole system ensures the promotion of such a mode of existence? Throughout the day, bludgeoned by the admen, we are encouraged to overconsume, although the consequences for the environment are concealed from us. We are engaged in a race for possessions that seems to be endless. Thus the Japanese now produce so many television sets that they no longer know who to sell them to. But world industry is not slow in finding a solution to the problem. Standards are changed, high definition is created, the old stock must be renewed. And the planet must 'change gear' with enthusiasm. In every field, the rich countries of today are swamped by a plethora of superfluous objects.

Competition and profitability, those are the values that our modern age has contrived to get praised to the skies—heaven knows how. Now we are evolving in a world of sharks, hunters of heads or premiums, 'raiders' and vicious takeover bids. Every sort of blow is legal and the man without the soul of a 'killer' is doomed to failure. On the other hand, one can only feign astonishment and disquiet when a society founded on such values begets an even bloodier, more real violence, which establishes itself in the streets of every metropolis. 'The fathers have eaten sour grapes, and the children's teeth are set on edge,' the Old Testament tells us. Suburban violence is matched by the institutional warfare which enables some to settle their accounts with others under the aegis of international interventions. We have sold arms cheaply to the most dubious regimes, the Americans offer them for sale on the open market, and everyone pretends to be offended when the buyer has the bad taste to make use of them!

Today corpses crowd our television screens and we no longer take any notice. If a traveller from the last century came across our TV news, he would not doubt for a moment that he had fallen into the midst of the Apocalypse. Try it for yourself. Run back over the news of the past year. You will see the conflicts in Yugoslavia, the drug-connected assaults in Colombia, the discovery of charnel-houses in Ruanda and Cambodia, the bloodthirsty uprisings in Zaire and Los Angeles, ethnic clashes in the four corners of the Earth, and so on. Not to mention the ever more alarming health bulletin on our planet, with its approaching shortages and famines in Somalia and the Sudan. All of this increased by cries of distress from the shattered populations, against a background of mounting fanaticism. The dangers increase, the warnings multiply and yet we take no notice.

*

Faced with such inertia, I find it a little too facile to accuse the media, whose subtitles and images make the horror commonplace. We are the ones who have lost our capacity to be horrified. I even ask myself if the word 'televiewer' does not encourage the confusing of reality with fiction. Everything becomes a mere spectacle, as if the main news slot represented the space for tragedy, soon forgotten in the amusements that follow, and which we call stupid, even though we are taking part in a ratings poll. We are amazed by ridiculous exploits (when will someone cross the Atlantic in a salad shaker?); we adore the bogus heroes, those idols that the Bible called nothings who are good for nothing. To paraphrase a Nobel Prizewinner, we are confronted with a generation that knows 'the fair price of everything and the true value of nothing.'

Faced with such falsehoods, how can we judge the urgency of the situation, be aware of the alarm signals, although they are already there, under our eyes? Remember Jesus Christ's words to the Pharisees(Matt. 16:2—3):

When it is evening ye say, It will be fair weather: for the sky is red. And in the morning, It will be foul weather today: for the sky is red and lowring. O ye hypocrites, ye can discern the face of the sky; but can ye not discern the signs of the times?

*

The signs of the Times . . . Yet originally television claimed to be a window on the world for us. Too often since then it is no more than a lantern-show mirage that lures us with soulless oases. It draws viewers in a slow downward spiral, a hypnotic helix condemning them to apathy while the fate of mankind is in the balance outside. I have already mentioned the strange epitaph found in an English cemetery on a sixteenth-century gravestone, which says that when images look alive and seem to be animated by their own movements . . . then half the World will be engulfed in blood. After radio, will television represent the famous Beast in the Revelation of St John, which will reign over the Earth, subduing men, before the end of Time?

Elsewhere I have recalled the shock I felt when visiting New York for the first time in the Sixties. In the heart of the city, on the façade of a skyscraper, I saw three enormous luminous figures. Three sixes— that is, 666: the encoded name given to the beast in Revelation about which so many questions have been asked!

I stood there, stock-still in front of this number, unable to understand its presence on the wall. Then I was told that it was the hertzian frequency chosen for the first radio broadcast . . .

All of a sudden I had the feeling that everything in my way of looking at things was falling into place. As far as I was concerned, there was absolutely no doubt that the hertzian waves, baptised with the number of the Beast, represented his means of propaganda. First radio, then television: 'And he had power to give life unto the image of the beast, that the image of the beast should . . . speak', wrote St John. This image which is animated (therefore moves) and speaks, what else is it but the televisual image, if not (also) that of all the information and electronic communication networks now at our disposal?

Please do not misunderstand me. I am not claiming that television and information processing are inventions of the devil, nor that their animators and technicians are Satan's henchmen. I am saying that the ways of the Demon are also hard to fathom, and that Evil has managed to find fantastic means of propagation in our badly managed modernism. At first, these inventions, like all those of science, had obvious positive aspects and even the possibility of noble projects. Everything that encourages dialogue and communication can bring men together, and the educational, professional or simply entertainment advantages of this new technology are undeniable. Except for one thing. We have not been wary enough of the Beast who approaches in disguise the better to seduce, counting on human weaknesses and aberrations. His primary goal was to subdue the human race. He has virtually succeeded. Today television programmes and data banks form gigantic spider's webs that crisscross the whole planet, like the electromagnetic currents awakened by the Sons of Belial in the past. None of us can claim to escape them. 'Who is like unto the Beast? Who is able to make war with him?' asks the Revelation of St John (13:4 and 7). '. . . power was given him over all kindreds, and tongues, and nations.'

No doubt I shall be accused of archaicism and of being an old-fashioned prophet of doom because of this disclosure, and yet . . . I am not the only one to hold these views. Intellectuals, writers, scholars and priests have already denounced the poisoning of minds by the media and control of individuals by information processing. Sometimes, the press and television themselves indulge in self-criticism. But these warnings have no effect.

Nevertheless, don't we have cause to shiver when we see what is in store for us? We know, for example, that we have all been indexed many times on a computer. A magnetic credit card has become our passport in the world. Without its code we can do nothing. What do we read in Revelation? '(The Beast) causeth all, both small and great, free and bound, to receive a mark in their right hand, or in their foreheads. And that no man might buy or sell, save he had the mark, or the name of the beast, or the number of his name.' You will say that this is an exaggerated interpretation? Recently, in view of the increase in the theft of credit cards, banks all over the world studied the projected idea of an electronic bug which would be inserted into the fingers of the hand and would enable everyone to make their purchases, but also open their car or house doors. The credit card would become biological.

As for the media, we have long wished to believe in the objectivity of their information, but since the Romanian revolution and the Gulf War, we have lost many of our illusions. We are entirely manipulated, at one end of the chain or the other, by a formidable mechanical potential for disinformation and the creation of fanaticism. What power will be strong enough to counterbalance the fourth power? Several times the Old Testament curses those who 'cause my people to err by their lies . . . Hearken not! . . . they make you vain . . . they speak a vision out of their own heart and not out of the mouth of the Lord.'

What's more, isn't the Beast appearing more and more in broad daylight? Everywhere we see the triumph of a cynicism which has nothing philosophic about it, but if anything is devoted to promoting vulgarity and indifference. Who still dares to claim that audiovisual communication is the ideal place for the discussion of ideas and different opinions? Cut off from reality, the 'interveners' only pretend to debate, seeing that they are all basically in agreement on the maintenance of the status quo and the privileges they all enjoy.

Shall I still be accused of blackening the picture if I deplore seeing young people today leave their books for the consoles of video games? What parent has not been shaken by the hallucinated gaze of his children mesmerised by the infernal clicking of these electronic images? Today we learn that their 'abuse' is dangerous to health and sometimes causes epileptic fits.

Are we heading towards a lobotomised mankind? Am I wrong to worry when I hear the information technicians talk of the next stage, which is that of 'virtual reality'? Viewers will become actors but in an imaginary way. With a hat-cum-bandage over their eyes, their bodies equipped with sensitive feelers, they will actually enter into the image in three dimensions, touch objects in it, and live a more or less programmed adventure with partners of their choice. This process opens up extraordinary prospects in the field of games and integral illusion. You will be able to play tennis, visit Beijing or experience your wildest erotic fantasies . . . without ever leaving your armchair. This is all very logical. Individual happiness must find its ultimate consummation in solitary pleasure. But that pleasure will involve the loss of mobility and lucidity. Could the Beast of Revelation have dreamt of a better means of control than this dream machine? People will no longer live except as phantasms. The triumph of degradation, the absolute opium, the arrival of robotised man . . .

*

That is how the reign of the Beast might be established (provided that it has not already begun). At least those are the images and fears that the number 666 has inspired in me. Recently, my interpretation has been completed by another interesting fact. I learnt that 666-666 was the number of the telephone line connecting President Nixon with Neil Armstrong, the first man to set foot on the Moon. We have come back to the idea of hertzian waves, but add to it the notion of human pride. Has not man repeated the sin of the builders of the Tower of Babel by treading lunar soil? Has he not put all his efforts into showing that he was no longer dependent on this Blue Planet, which had been put in his charge?

Of course this remains a personal interpretation, far from unique of its kind. The number of the Beast has always given rise to many theories, from the most learned to the most farfetched. Gematria, a part of the cabal based on connections between

mathematics and the alphabet, claimed that 666 hid
the names of Nero and Caesar. Faithful to my concept of picking symbols out of a drawer, I personally
am inclined to accept various conclusions. At the
same time, I have always preferred simplicity. Sometimes we have to know it is right to opt for things of
the highest order and that is why I am amazed that
the most obvious explanation has not been given
pride of place, the one which justifies all the vari-
ations. Genesis says that in the beginning was the
Word. It was the Word of God that gave birth to the
world: it is the principle of life and love communicated at the Creation. At the end of Time, on the
other hand, Number appears (in opposition to 7, 6
is antiperfection, Evil). So 666 would signify number
taking precedence over language, suddenly deprived
of its capacity to create Being. Today, the 'informis-
ation' of society is completing this reversal. It is the
victory of robotic reasoning over aesthetic thought,
it is the replacement of society with a human face
by the frigid dictatorship of machines.

Is there still a way of influencing this disastrous
evolutionary trend? What can we do except 'take care
not to be surprised' by the day of the catastrophe.
That is what Luke invites us to do in the New Testament (21:34–35): 'And take heed to yourselves, lest at
any time your hearts be overcharged with surfeiting,
and drunkenness, and cares of this life, and so that
day come upon you unawares. For as a snare shall
it come on all them that dwell on the face of the whole
earth.'

*   *   *

Many people sense this threat in a confused way.
Then follows a feeling of malaise which paralyses
them, a deep irrational anguish that neither ordi-
nary medicine nor psychiatry can cure. And as they
cannot bear to live in doubt, as they must have

immediate happiness, at any price, they turn to the 'sorcerers'. A paradox of the end of the age of Pisces: people jib at belief in God (except in cases of fanaticism which I shall mention later), but rush to consult the false prophets. Hoping for miracles that they want solely to ensure their own comfort, they open the door to charlatans of every calibre, from the weirdest to the most dangerous. Oriental pseudo-sages, homegrown gurus, suburban bonzes, spiritual DIY-men, arthritic yogis, travelling circus witches, telepathists of abracadabra, quack bonesetters . . . the choice is all too wide. With varying degrees of cynicism, they all exploit the angst that characterises our 'era of the void', to use a modern philosopher's expression.

Of course, not all these false prophets are ill-intentioned at first. Some of them (they are rare) sincerely believe that they are working to relieve their contemporaries' moral distress. In Paris in the Sixties, one might meet in some café or other a certain Angel Cyclamen who said he was sent by the Lord to save the world. His technique was tenderness. He claimed that soon a new continent would emerge in the Pacific and would be shaped like a heart.

Other bogus magi expose themselves to ridicule like this, for example the worshippers of the Small Pyramid, who walk around San Francisco all day wearing pointed hats to capture spatial waves. Or again, those devotees of the Onion, who venerate that vegetable as the symbol of the eternity of the human soul.

The oddest (and the most disturbing) thing is that all these charlatans have houses of their own and even hold meetings where one can take part in conferences on 'broccoli and the anti-stress struggle' or 'the cabalistic reading of Who's Who', between two stages of initiation into prophetic iridology or the magnetisation of eggs in aspic. Don't laugh, I'm only slightly exaggerating.

The trouble is that the joke often turns into a nightmare. No doubt surprised by the credulity of their clientele, the false prophets turn themselves into merchants at the temple. 'The prophets thereof divine for money', Micah (3:11) tells us in the Old Testament. 'Every one is given to covetousness', adds Jeremiah (6:13). If they convince their victims of the folly of material possessions, it is only to get their own hands on them more easily. In the Gospel according to St Matthew (7:15), Christ warns against the 'false prophets, which come to you in sheep's clothing, but inwardly they are ravening wolves'. How many gurus professing poverty as the path to wisdom ride in Rolls Royces and make a royal progress through the world living in luxury!

Possessed by delusions of grandeur, these megalomaniacs have churches and colossal statues built at great expense, for their own glory. Drunk with the power of the influence they find they hold over the human mind, they lose no time in using it for the worst. Whether they are of a financial, spiritual or affective order, their manipulations can drag the weakest to the verge of madness. Or even death. Remember the Temple of the People, installed in the Guyanese jungle. Its founder, Jim Jones, drove the thousand members of his sect to collective suicide. 'The starving wolves rush down from the mountain and devour the sheep which they tear to pieces even in the midst of their fold,' the prophecy of Prémol tells us.

Today there are hundreds of sects in France and thousands in the United States. It is impossible to draw up a complete list, as new ones are springing up every day. Their proliferation is itself the sign of the imminence of the end of Time: 'People will venerate false gods in false ashrams in which fasts, pilgrimages, penances, donation of one's goods and austerity in the name of self-styled religions will be arbitrarily decreed,' we read in the *Vishnu Purana*. All these false prophets pave the way for the one who will be their master, he who will carry diabolical seduction to its peak: the Antichrist. If the occult powers are summoned for long enough, they finally reply. And those who had had ideas of taming them will soon become their slaves. For one does not play with incantations with impunity.

*

For all that, should we throw stones at those who let themselves be lulled by some of these malevolent sirens? They are usually disorientated and vulnerable people, especially young ones. If sects have begun to sprout in this way, it is mainly because there was a space to fill. Are they not happy to fill the void left by the desertion of the established Church?

I assert that the established Church has failed in her task. And that she is not up to the critical situation in which we live. Why should we be surprised? She is the same Church that has falsified the teaching of the early Christians for centuries—she who, from council to encyclical, has applied herself to misrepresenting Christ's message of love. We have seen her give the worst of examples, among others those of the Inquisition and the luxury adopted by unscrupulous prelates.

No doubt this slow perversion was inevitable. The cosmic law, which churches do not escape, provides that everything which has been created undergoes the erosion of time. Religion of the age of Pisces, Christianity as we know it has run its race, worn out, emptied of its substance. It should be said in its defence that it was severely tested during recent centuries. The humanism of the Renaissance diminished the divine to magnify the individual; the Age of Enlightenment glorified human rationality, and our own epoch has finally ensured the triumph of scientism and atheism. Today, as a disconsolate André Froissard can remark, 'the Christian universe has plunged so deeply into oblivion that its shipwreck no longer makes waves.'

The Pope seems to be resigned to going down with his ship. Instead of introducing the reform necessary for the passage from one era to another, instead of using arguments against moral dereliction that would suit the period, the Church is clinging rigidly to its old positions. The timid exhortations in the contemporary Mass to shake hands in the peace of Christ are not enough for a new assessment of 'Christian charity'. The faithful are entitled to hope for a more scrupulous reading of the texts, a vision stripped of all will to power. In this respect, they undoubtedly expected much from the 'new' catechism. All they found in it, for the most part, was the repetition of worn-out ideas. Worse still, the very few innovations formally contradicted the founding principles of the original Church. Thus the death penalty has been recognised as legitimate in certain cases. Is that the only means that has been found to win back the disillusioned members of the Catholic Church: an ignoble concession to the barbarism of the epoch? Has the papacy forgotten that one of the Ten Commandments demands that 'Thou shalt not kill'? Henceforth she deserves to heed Matthew's warning: 'Judge not, that ye be not judged.'

More conservatism when the catechism lays down as dogma that 'all forms of divination are to be rejected'. I am the first to denounce excesses and charlatanism, but I remember what Paul himself said in the First Epistle to the Thessalonians (5:20–21): 'despise not prophesyings. Prove all things; hold fast that which is good.' And remember this superb passage from Peter in his Second Epistle (1:19): 'We have also a more sure word of prophecy; whereunto ye do well that ye take heed, as unto a light that shineth in a dark place, until the day dawn, and the day star arise in your hearts.'

*

I lay emphasis on Christianity because it is the predominant religion in the age of Pisces. Belonging as I do to this age (in my present reincarnation at least), I have always felt myself profoundly Christian. But Christian as it was in the beginning of Time, holder of a message of love, not of extermination, dominance or hate. Now, like Judaism and Islam, at the dawn of the great upheaval lying in wait for us, Christianity finds itself tempted, here and there, by a form of fundamentalism. Rome condemns this attitude, of course, but Rome does not seek to return to the purity of the early Christians. The Revelation of St John opens with a severe recall to order: 'All the churches shall know that I am he which searcheth the reins and hearts: and I will give unto every one of you according to your works.'

Still in the same prophetic book, we read about Queen Jezebel, who led her husband away from worship of the true God: 'I gave her space to repent of her fornication; and she repented not.' Rome, the modern Jezebel, will pay dearly for her blindness and obstinacy. St John again: 'Alas, alas that great city . . . in one hour is she made desolate.'

This destruction seems to be very close, if we are to believe the extraordinary prophecy of St Malachy. This primate of the Irish church, friend of the illustrious St Bernard of Clairvaux, lived in the first half of the twelfth century. In the prophecy that bears his name, he established the line of 111 popes who would succeed each other from Celestine II in 1143 until the end of time. The prophecy actually consisted of 111 Latin mottos, each one concerning a sovereign pontiff. Here are some examples showing the warning nature of these mottos. The hundredth, referring to Gregory XIV, Pope from 1831 to 1846, was '*De Balnae Etruriae*'—'from Balnes in Etruria'. Gregory XIV belonged to the religious order of the Camaldolites, whose centre was in the town of . . . Balnes, in Etruria.

Clement XIII, elected in 1758, was allotted (in the twelfth century, remember!) the motto '*Rosa Umbriae*'. Now before becoming pope, he was governor of a town in Umbria, the symbol of which was the rose. His successor was to be '*Ursus Velox*'. This was Clement XIV, scion of a family whose arms depicted a bear at full speed. Innocent XII, Pope from 1691 to 1700, was named by the motto 'The rake at the door'. Well, his name was none other than Rastello, 'rake' in Italian.

As for more recent popes . . . John XXIII (1958–63), according to St Malachy, was '*Pastor nautaque*'— 'shepherd and mariner'. He had been patriarch of Venice, city of mariners! The motto of his successor Paul VI (1963–1978) was '*Flora florum*', the 'flower of flowers', that is the lily. His arms consisted of three lilies and in addition he was a native of Florence, whose symbol is the lily. '*De medietate lunae*' (half of the moon) was applied to John Paul I. He was elected at the time of the half-moon and died a month later. So his reign lasted only from one half-moon to another.

As for John Paul II, he is '*De labore solis*', 'the work of the sun'. Will the significance of this motto appear later at the end of his reign? Or is it an allusion to his indefatigable work as a traveller in a world on which the sun never sets? Indeed, no other pope has travelled the world so much, from one continent to another, kissing the ground everywhere as if to ask its pardon for his own impotence. He should take care! Certain quatrains by Nostradamus (which I have quoted before) forecast the assassination of the Polish pope, something that has very nearly happened already.

On top of all this, according to St Malachy, John Paul II will be the 110th pope out of the 111 foretold, or 112. I shall explain the reason for this 'supplementary' pope who has no 'surname' in the prophecy. At all events, there will only be one or two more popes before the Apocalypse. Will Christianity (as it is conceived of today) come to an end? A disturbing prophecy by St Anselm puts us on our guard: 'Woe to the time when the letter 'K' shall be exalted in the walls of Rome!' Every one knows that Jean Paul II's Polish Christian name is Karol . . .

What would happen then? John Paul II's successor is described as '*De gloriae olivae*', 'the glory of the olive-tree'.

Some people recognise that as a special sign. The olive-tree is the traditional symbol of the Jewish people. This 'glory of the olive-tree' might stand for the accession of a Jew to the supreme throne of the Catholic Church. After all, we already have in France a bishop who was once of the Hebraic persuasion.

Having said that, I do not think that the 'glory of the olive-tree' will be the last sovereign pontiff. For at the end of his long list Malachy explains: 'During the last persecution of the Holy Roman Church, Peter the Roman will reign. He will pasture his flock in the midst of many tribulations. Once these tribulations are over, the town of the seven hills (Rome) will be destroyed and the redoubtable judge will judge his people.' Should we conclude from this that Christians will again be persecuted for their beliefs and the exercise of their religion? It is possible. But what is sure, in any case, is that this religion is dying because it has betrayed its nature. Cathedrals are profaned by hordes of tourists, the young are no longer interested in God, or they turn towards sects which refer to Christ in an exotic and profane way. 'When I shall return to this earth,' says the living Christ in the New Testament, 'will there still be anyone left to believe in me?' St Paul himself has warned us that there must be aspostasy before the day of the great punishment. Henceforth, everything is ready for the last act.

*   *   *

'The Church will have a terrible crisis. The holy faith of God being forgotten, each individual will choose to be guided by himself and be superior to his fellow men.' This prophecy, which sums up the irreligion of our society and the arrogant egoism of men, is taken from the message given by the Virgin to two young shepherds near La Salette, in the Dauphiné Alps in 1846. Other Marian revelations were to follow. Take Amsterdam in 1946: 'Religion will have to wage a hard battle. People will seek to destroy it: this will be done with such refinement that no one, or hardly anyone, will notice.'

The Virgin has appeared to men at all times and particularly to children, because of the purity of their souls. But never have these Marian apparitions been as frequent as in the nineteenth century. Rationalists have tried to explain these 'phenomena' as sudden flashes of religious faith among the population. Should we not rather attribute them to the Virgin's anxiety when faced with the growing atheism which characterises the end of Kali Yuga? Are they not yet another sign of the imminence of great tribulations? It all seems as if the Virgin was making a last effort to warn us, to exhort us to return to the path of God, if there is still time. Mother-goddess, she is above all compassion, she intercedes for us and tries to open our eyes to our options in the face of catastrophe.

During the last two centuries, several hundred

Marian apparitions have been confirmed from all over the world. Many have taken place in France and Italy, and some have been recognised by the Church herself. In 1830 the Virgin announced to a young nun in the Rue du Bac in Paris: 'The whole world will be disturbed by misfortunes of every kind.' There were similar warnings at Lourdes in 1858 and at Fatima in 1917, not to mention at Banneux in Belgium (1933) and at Beauraing, and so on.

Everywhere the message is the same. The Virgin rebukes men for their negligence, their vanity and their lack of spiritual life. 'The heads, the leaders of the people of God have neglected prayer and penance and the Demon has obscured their intelligence', said the divine Mother at La Salette. 'Let the bishops act! Let them order their priests to turn to young people to save them from this modern paganism,' she announced in Amsterdam. 'This materialist world is hastening to its doom.'

The Marian apparitions are a final exhortation, a supplication full of loving pity, although on occasion it may assume the accents of a terrible threat: 'If my people does not want to submit, I am forced to let loose the arm of my son . . .'

All the prophecies have warned us time and time again. Are we going to remain deaf and blind right up to the end? When the day comes, we shall have no attenuating circumstances to offer. 'The banquet of them that stretched themselves shall be removed,' says the prophet Amos.

Chapter 6

THE TRUMPETS OF THE APOCALYPSE

A warning concerning this chapter

God is my witness to all the suffering and anguish I went through while writing the lines that follow. Did I have the right to pen them? But there is nothing fictional about them. They are simply the result of decades of reading and meditation in the light of the ancient Wisdom, confirming the events that were shown me on the Seventh Vibratory Plane and which motivated my return to Earth. For an instant a feeling of divine terror made me doubt the need to reveal them, but while I was writing these pages, the Twenty-Four Elders arrived and stood around my table, pointing authoritatively to the sheet of paper and giving me the order: 'Write!'

I bowed to their command. But it was frightening. So I have a message for any over-fragile readers: if you have not the strength to open your eyes and see, then skip these pages which are intended for brave souls who will better understand how urgent it is for them to redouble their prayers so that all the horrors may be diminished.

When the fishing boat shall be lost.

Nostradamus

Now we have come to the last act, the act of the end of Time. Impossible to conceive of it without one question springing to mind, a question formulated in the 129th Sura of the Koran: 'They will ask you, saying: when will this fatal hour come?' Here the Islamic text urges the Prophet to be prudent. His role in fact is not to give the date of the end of the world: 'What dost thou know about it? Its date is known only to God. Thou art only charged to warn those who dread it.'

The fact is that anyone who claimed to calculate our eschatological judgement day accurately would have to be very rash or presumptuous. In the New Testament Matthew also asks us to abandon any idea of a prediction: 'But of that day and hour knoweth no man, no, not the angels of heaven, but my Father only.'

Bear that in mind. No one can or should presume to predict the hour when the last trumpet of the Apocalypse will sound. However, by comparing the prophecies and the History of mankind, one can say that all the stages heralding the Apocalypse have now been passed. Yes, our civilisation has moved away from faith and tradition. Yes, we have turned towards false doctrines. Yes, we have preferred easily available pleasures to the narrow path, violence to respect for others. Yes, we have destroyed the Earth.

'Tremble,' says the Virgin of La Salette, 'you who profess to serve Jesus Christ, and who in your hearts adore yourselves, tremble, for God will deliver you to your enemies.'

Don't recent decades correspond to the beginning of the sufferings (*initia dolorum*) which all the prophecies mention? Hasn't this century which, not without reason, has been called the most violent in human history, gathered together all the horrors of which man is capable? The time has come to pay the bill for our innumerable crimes and errors. The karma accumulated by mankind has reached a weight never equalled before and the Earth cannot support the yoke of this human plague much longer.

The pages that follow paint a rather gloomy picture of our destiny. So much so that I may be falling under the spell of this sally by Jean Rostand, who called himself 'very optimistic about the future of pessimism'. Nevertheless I think I am lucid rather than pessimistic. For a distant glimmer, on which I keep my eye fixed, has constantly pierced the darkness that assails me. And I know we shall not have too much of this guide to lead us through the great tribulations to come.

Of course, these woes only make up a probable scenario . . . unfortunately confirmed by most of the prophecies. Now as we have seen in the course of this book and down the centuries, these predictions have turned out to be remarkably reliable. What blindness still makes us refuse to believe in them? In my case, this ostrich head policy is all the more impossible because the prophecies are matched by personal visions and I cannot forget them or the evidence they contain. On the contrary, these visions haunt me more intensely every day, undoubtedly to warn me how close they are to being realised.

Naturally, we cannot know exactly when the arm of the Lord will fall on us, but we should remember the sentence from the Koran aimed at all those who ask themselves about the proximity of the end of Time: 'On the day when they shall see it, they will feel as if they have only remained on earth one evening or one morning.'

*   *   *

Haven't we already heard the three knocks before the curtain rises, or the first two at least? As in the theatre, the tragedy of the Apocalypse has its coded preliminaries. Here, the raising of the curtain is apparently to be preceded by tremendous historical events: the three planetary crises formed by the 1914–18 War, the 1939–45 War and the Third World War still to come. All three have been prophesied. As the first two have happened, the third seems highly likely, to say the least. Perhaps it has already begun . . .

In the tenth century, an abbess who became famous for her visionary trances lived in the convent of Gandersheim in Saxony. In a manuscript entitled *Tuba Seculorum*, the 'Bugle of the Centuries', Sister Hroswitte described the combatants in a vast conflict: 'The peoples will fall under thee, Germany, and thy power will be so great that the whole world will ally themselves against thee.' And the abbess gave a precise date for this event: 'when the 255th Pope shall die.' This 255th pope was none other than Pius X, who died in 1914!

Written in the seventeenth century, the previously mentioned prophecy of the Unknown Monk looked on the twentieth century as 'the strangest of all the centuries for men will be mad with themselves and the world and will destroy each other.' After a preliminary war 'in which bullets will fall from the sky', the Unknown Monk announced a 'second war during which nearly the whole of creation will be convulsed. Great disasters of fortune and goods will come about and many tears will be shed, men will be without souls and without pity.' Obviously these warnings were not taken seriously until afterwards. Today it is a Third World War that threatens us. By an unlikely coincidence, the third knock before the curtain rises has struck in the same place as the first. In 1914, Europe blazed up as a result of the assassination of Archduke Franz Ferdinand by a Serbian student at Sarajevo. Today Sarajevo is once again highly topical. Will the powder keg of the Balkans, made so unstable by a mosaic of nationalities and religions, be the hub of a planetary conflict, as it was at the beginning of the century?

At all events, that is what Nostradamus unequivocally predicts in his Fourth Century, quatrain 82: 'The constellation draws near, coming from Esclavonia.' Esclavonia is none other than the ancient name of Slavonia, a northern province of former Yugoslavia. In the same quatrain the wise man of Salon-de-Provence adds: 'The great flame will never be extinguished.' Today, every observer fears an extension of the Serbo-Croat war. Will an intervention by the great powers burst the abscess or set fire to the gunpowder? The decision is difficult. In the meantime, we allow the crimes to be perpetrated and the fire spreads. Shall we be able to put it out in time?

Another false coincidence? It was in Yugoslavia that one of the most recent apparitions of the Virgin took place, in the village of Mejdugorje, only a few dozen kilometres from Sarajevo. The apparitions began in June 1981 on a hill in the neighbourhood and continued in the village church. Several people, in a state of ecstasy, distinctly saw the silhouette of the Mother-Goddess. An interesting detail is that the clothing of the Virgin who appeared has changed down the years. Formerly she wore a dazzling white dress, or a blue mantle dotted with gold spangles. All she wears now is a simple dress of black sackcloth, as if to summon us to austerity and penance, and she is weeping. At Mejdugorje the Virgin conveyed messages and secrets about future events. 'I am come to you as Queen of peace to tell the world that its health is in danger.' The little town soon became a favourite place of pilgrimage; the faithful flocked there in their hundreds of thousands. Nevertheless, in 1985 the bishops gave their verdict on the case: they refused to recognise the visions. No doubt it was feared that they would discredit the Church's authority.

The voice of peace was gagged once again. You would have thought that we were determined not to hear anything! We know that Fatima's third and last secret has not yet been divulged, even though we suspect that it contains the announcement of the Third World War. The popes, sole holders of the message, have obstinately refused to make its exact contents known. To some extent, we can understand their desire not to spread panic, but surely the peoples of the world should be warned?

Military preparations resound on all sides. 'The horrible clash of arms!' cries St Caesarius of Arles. After proclaiming multiple pogroms and diasporas (those of the Second World War?), the prophecy of Prémol laments as follows: 'Is such a hecatomb, O Lord, not enough to appease your wrath? By no means. What are these sounds of arms, these cries of war and terror borne by the four winds?'

Neverthethess, enormous hope was aroused in 1989, after the Iron Curtain fell. The two Great Powers had put an end to their rivalry, the risks of a widespread conflict seemed to be averted once and for all. We celebrated the arrival of a 'new world order' that would guarantee our security. Then why have we not reread the messages of the Virgin at La Salette? Before the war actually breaks out, she tells us, 'there will be a false peace in the world, people will think only of enjoying themselves.' All of us believed in this 'false peace', we cheered when the Berlin wall was knocked down. But disenchantment quickly followed, the 'pax americana' drawing us into a period fraught with danger, as demonstrated by the Gulf War that Nostradamus had predicted: 'Under the opposite Babylonic climate, great will be the effusion of blood, so that land and sea, air, sky, will be as one.'

We are discovering to our horror that a good number of lesser powers have the capacity to unleash catastrophe. Do we even know exactly which states possess atomic weapons? Now that the status quo of the Cold War is at an end, we are right in the middle of a zone of serious convulsions and nationalist claims. With extraordinary prescience, Nostradamus picked out this turning-point in the 57th quatrain of his Second Century: 'The great wall will fall before the conflict.'

*   *   *

One of the characteristics of the Balkans is that they form the place where two civilisations, one Nordic and Slav, the other Arabian, meet and friction arises. Mortal enemies for a very long time, they have become reconciled in the course of this century. Thus, the last few decades have seen the Russians provide logistic support to the Arab nations fighting against Israel.

In my opinion it is there, in the Near and Middle East, that the second focus (after Serbia) of the next war is situated. The first target, as we have seen, is the town of Jerusalem. Jesus Christ himself predicted it in the Gospel according to St Luke (21:24): 'Jerusalem shall be trodden down of the Gentiles, until the times of the Gentiles be fulfilled.' The capital of Israel is also condemned by the prophecy of Prémol: 'A thunderclap opened the clouds, and I saw Jerusalem under a terrifying tempest, and its walls had fallen under blows from the battering-ram, and blood flowed in the streets: for the enemy had become masters of the city.' 'The abomination of desolation' will begin with this occupation.

Arabs and peoples of the former Soviet Union will contract a military alliance, the former made fanatical by religious solidarity, the latter goaded by misery and the mustiness of a Communism thought moribund, but which only awaits the chance to rise again from its ashes, on the dunghill of social and economic decomposition. 'Arabia and Hungary will take the same course,' Nostradamus tells us in the Tenth Century, quatrain 63. Before that (Fifth Century, quatrain 73), he announced the persecution of the Church and Christian peoples when 'Arabs and Poles will be allies.'

'The Oriental will emerge from his seat,' Nostradamus warns us again (Second Century, quatrain 29). Now this 'oriental' means both the people who come from the East and those who come from the Orient.

'Watch and listen,' said the Virgin Mary at Amsterdam, 'the Orient against the Occident. Europe, take care!'

In 1792, Joanna Southcott, the young daughter of a Devonshire farmer, had a sudden and brief revelation concerning the end of Time: 'When the oriental war shall come, know ye that the end is fatal.'

Two armies, one coming from the East and the North, the other from the South and the Orient, will converge in the direction of Europe. In the Old Testament, the prophet Ezekiel (chapter 38) gives a detailed description of the array of the enemy troops, whom he calls Gog and Magog, and reminds us that their forces will be armed by God.

Behold, I am against thee, O Gog, the chief prince of Meshech and Tubal: And I will turn thee back, and put hooks into thy jaws, and I will bring thee forth, and all thine army, horses and horsemen, all of them clothed with all sorts of armour, even a great company with bucklers and shields, all of them handling swords: Persia, Ethiopia and Libya with them; all of them with shield and helmet: Gomer, and all his bands; the house of Togarmah of the north quarters, and all his bands: and many people with thee. Be thou prepared, and prepare for thyself, thou, and all thy company that are assembled unto thee, and be thou a guard unto them.

After many days thou shalt be visited: in the latter years thou shalt come back into the land that is brought back from the sword, and is gathered out of many people, against the mountains of Israel, which have been always waste: but it is brought forth out of the nations, and they shall dwell safely all of them. Thou shalt ascend and come like a storm, thou shalt be like a cloud to cover the land, thou, and all thy bands, and many people with thee.

All those countries delivered from war and reunited in a multinational framework—surely that is Europe? Or does it mean the United Nations?

*

The Revelation of St John, the last book in the New Testament, devoted to man's ultimate fate, gives us a striking description of the invaders already mentioned in the Bible. We know that his narrative shows John of Patmos rising into the heavens to contemplate from above the grandiose and tragic scenes of the end of Time. The Book of Divine Intentions is revealed to the apostle who opens its seven seals one by one. On opening the seventh seal, he discovers the punishment with which God will visit mankind. Seven trumpets will sound the different stages. When the fifth trumpet sounds, 'locusts' rise from the smoke. But they are purely symbolic locusts which inevitably suggest our aircraft and other machines used in modern wars!

'And the shapes of the locusts were like unto horses prepared unto battle; and on their heads were as it were crowns like gold, and their faces were as the faces of men . . . And they had breast-plates, as it were breastplates of iron; and the sound of their wings was as the sound of chariots of many horses running to battle. And they had tails like unto scorpions, and there were stings in their tails.

When the sixth trumpet was heard, a new army appeared,

for to slay the third part of men . . . The number of the army of the horsemen were two hundred thousand thousand . . . having breastplates of fire, and of jacinth, and brimstone: and the heads of the horses were as the heads of lions . . . By these three was the third part of men killed, by the fire, and by the smoke, and by the brimstone, which issued out of their mouths.

A countless army, formidably equipped, and all the more irresistible because it will march on many fronts. While the Russians will sweep through Germany and the whole of northern Europe, the Moslems will advance by means of several Mediterranean offensives. 'Persia turns to invade Macedonia,' Nostradamus tells us (Second Century, quatrain 96). How far will they go? 'The great camel will come and drink the waters of the Danube and the Rhine,' the prophet adds (Fifth Century, quatrain 68). The camel symbolises the Arab army which is to join up with the Slav troops on the banks of these two great European rivers.

Farther west, the Moslems will retread the paths along which the ancient Moors made their conquests. Spain will be invaded, according to the 55th quatrain of Nostradamus's Fifth Century:

> In the country of Arabia Felix
> one skilled in Mohammedan law will be born
> to trouble Spain; the conquest of Granada
> and more land by the Lygustic people
> coming from the sea.

The Iberian peninsula will be subjected to Islamic law. All attempts at resistance will be crushed. 'Far from Iberia to the kingdom of Granada, the Cross driven back by the Mohammedan people', we read in the Third Century, quatrain 20.

Italy will suffer the same fate (First Century, quatrain 9):

> The Punic heart will come from the East
> to harass Hadria and the heirs of Romulus,
> accompanied by the Libyan fleet.
> Melite temples and those of neighbouring
> islands will be left empty.

There is no need for translation: the Punic heart stands for the Carthaginians, the North Africans who, irritated by the situation in the Adriatic, the sea washing Yugoslavia, and by the attitude of the popes 'inheriting' Rome, will send their fleet to assault Italy. Perhaps the Mélites are the 'melkites', the name the Moslems formerly gave to Catholics. Thus the war would empty the Christian churches and the islands of the Mediterranean.

But the main objective is the seat of the papacy.

Joachim de Flore, twelfth-century sage, poet and philosopher, predicted a heavy punishment for it: 'Rome, town bereft of all Christian discipline, is the source of all the abominations of Christianity; she it is who will first be stricken by the judgement of God.'

Giovanni di Vatiguerro prophesied that the sovereign pontiff would flee the Holy City in haste and that he and his companions would be lucky 'if they could find a place of refuge where each one and his own can eat aught but the bread of torment in this vale of tears.'

That confirms the prophetic vision which Pope Pius X had on his death-bed in 1914: 'I saw one of my successors who fled, straddling the bodies of his brothers. He will take refuge somewhere, incognito: and after a brief respite he will die a cruel death.' This hasty retreat, followed by the brutal death of the sovereign pontiff, is a feature of all the premonitions. And the pope in question is obviously Peter the Roman, the 112th in St Malachy's prophecy, the head of Christianity at the time of the 'ultimate persecution'.

*

Once Rome has been razed from top to bottom, the Moslems will pursue their way. 'He will cross over the Appenine mountains to see France: he will pierce through the sky, the waters and the snow and chastise everyone with his rod,' writes Nostradamus (Second Century, quatrain 29).

Divided and ill-prepared, France will be unable to defend herself against this invader. That is what this celebrated quatrain tells us:

> Through discord and French negligence
> Passage will be open to Mahomet,
> The Senois land and sea soaked with

> Blood, the Phocean port covered with
> sails and ships.

The Phocean port is obviously Marseilles invaded by
enemy ships. Simple geography will then make
France the point of convergence for all enemy bridge-
heads. The invader will arrive by the Pyrenees, by
sea, by Italy, the Balkans and Germany.

> France attacked in five parts by neglect,
> Tunisia, Algeria, aroused by the Persians:
> Leon, Seville, Barcelona in distress
> will have no fleet from the Venetians.

The Iraqis (Persians) will have incited the other Arab
nations, such as Tunisia and Algeria, to revolt. The
great Spanish towns will succumb, followed by the
French, unable to wait for help from Italy, herself
already under the yoke.

Paris will not be able to hold out for long. Its destruction is foretold everywhere. Giovanni di Vatiguerro
sees 'the capture, spoiling and devastating of the capital and mistress of the whole kingdom of the French'.
'Paris will be a real carnage,' says an anonymous nun
whose collected prophecies, published in 1882,
earned her the surname of 'the ecstatic of Tours'. The
town will suffer from fire and bloodshed, there will be
street by street and house by house fighting. The most
daring will seek refuge in cellars, sewers and the
countless caves and quarries underneath Paris. The
real punishment must wait a little longer.

After much beating about the bush, the Americans, a prey to internal disorder, will intervene in an
attempt to save Europe, or what is left of it. Then
will come the genuinely global war. Fighting will go
on everywhere: 'there will be disasters from North to
South, from South to West and from the Occident
to the Orient,' says the Virgin at Amsterdam.

No nation will be able to resist this infernal whirl-wind. Jeanne Le Royer, a nun who lived in the eigh-teenth century, had foretold that the arrival of the Antichrist would be preceded by bloodthirsty wars: 'Peoples will rise up against peoples, nations against nations, sometimes divided and sometimes united, to fight for or against the same party.'

At this stage of the conflict, alliances will be subject to unforeseeable reversals. War will no longer be solely a war of nation against nation, but a war of races, towns, tribes. All the prophecies predict this terrible deviation. Take this one from Prémol: 'Men and peoples have risen against each other. Wars, wars! Civil wars, foreign wars! What terrible clashes! All is death and mourning . . .'

The Virgin of La Salette was also terrified of these fratricidal combats: 'France, Italy, Spain and Eng-land will be at war. Blood will run in the streets. Frenchmen will fight with Frenchmen, Italian with Italian; then there will be a general war which will be appalling. There will be mutual killing and mass-acring even inside the houses.'

*

In the midst of this chaos the Almighty will suddenly intervene. Many prophecies emphasise the two-phased nature of the divine punishment. First the wars and revolutions, then the planetary cataclysm which will wipe out everything . . . or almost.

*   *   *

To punish men, God at first contented himself with bringing their warlike passions to a climax, doubt-less to make them face up to their monstrosity for the last time. The second phase is the 'vacuum-cleaning' of the devastated planet. The divine inter-vention will not be made, as some people naïvely imagine, in a 'personal' fashion. Let us forget once and for all our anthropomorphic conceptions of the celestial Almighty. Let us forget those cartoon pictures which explained the Flood by showing us a bearded, chubby-cheeked God spitting on the Earth.

The 'terrible shock' will take place in a very physical, material way, making use of the four elements: earth, air, water and above all fire. The last-named, as we have seen, will be the favourite instrument of the coming destruction.

The Chaldean Sibyl, a great soothsayer in Antiquity, made this threat in the past:

> If you do not listen to me, fire will descend on the Earth. Here are the signs that will announce it: at sunrise swords will be seen, terrible groanings and noises will be heard. Fire will consume the whole of the Earth, it will destroy the whole of the human race, all the towns, rivers and the sea; it will burn everything and reduce the world to a blackish dust.

What will be the actual cause of this fire? There are many scenarios. At the height of a world conflict, one naturally thinks of an atomic explosion. Short of resources, on the verge of defeat, some nations will take the risk of using this weapon, which is as devastating as it is suicidal, since it entails a counter-blow and chain reactions.

Written centuries and centuries ago, the prophetic Hindu texts have a strange echo in this respect. Thus the *Ramayana* offers us the vision of an 'unknown weapon, a thunder of fire, gigantic messenger of death, which reduced to ashes all the members of the race of Vrishnis and Andhakas.' This weapon appeared in the form of a 'single projectile charged with the power of the Universe. An incandescent smoke, like ten thousand suns, rose up in its splendour.' After the explosion, the Hindu text describes 'blueish clouds shaped like an egg or a luminous globe'. Is there a better description of the atomic mushroom cloud?

For my part, I do not in any way exclude this nuclear disaster. Any more than a gigantic earthquake 'such as had never been seen since men were on the earth' (Revelation). In 1992, there were no fewer than 70 deadly earthquakes: California, Indonesia, Egypt, Nicaragua . . . Add to that volcanoes becoming active again. The Earth is already groaning. In this case, the prophets' destructive force would be the molten lava.

Nevertheless, there is a danger that this earthquake might be just the 'simple' consequence of an even more formidable disaster: the entry into our atmosphere of an asteroid that would sweep the planet clean or even collide with it. When the prophets tackle the subject of 'signs of the end of Time', don't they speak of a comet visible to everyone? The comet might come much too close, as is suggested in the 41st quatrain of Nostradamus's Second Century:

> For seven days the great star will burn,
> the ash cloud will make two suns appear,
> the great mastiff will howl all night
> when the supreme pontiff shall change his
>   dwelling-place.

Here the visionary of Salon-de-Provence gives us a valuable chronological pointer. The second sun which threatens to burn everything on earth will make its appearance soon after the pope, chased away by the Arab invasion, has left Rome.

We find this comet again in the second secret of the Virgin of Fatima: 'When you shall see a night lit by a large unknown light, know that it is the sign that God gives you when the punishment of the world is near.' This message is echoed by the prophecy of the celebrated Italian soothsayer Giovanni di Vatiguerro: 'Numerous and very surprising signs will be seen in the sky. Stars will collide, that will be the signal for the destruction and massacre of nearly all mankind.' Then we have this revelation by the Virgin, who appeared to Veronica, a young American, at Bayside in New York State: 'The punishment which will be sent to mankind, my child, will be a great ball of fire that rushes through the sky and throws out gilded particles . . .'

A meteorite as signal and instrument of the divine wrath . . . When the Third World War is at its height, all we shall have to do is await the day, as Nostradamus (Tenth Century, quatrain 60) invites us, when 'the bearded star will appear towards the Little Bear, not far from Cancer.'

*

Ultimately the exact nature of the scourge matters little. What is certain is that everything will happen quickly, very quickly. All the prophecies agree on this point: the cataclysm will be 'instantaneous, of short duration, but terrible.' At the end of the eighteenth century, in Italy, Anna Maria Taigi, a nun in the order of the Holy Trinity, announced that: 'He who shall open his window out of curiosity at the moment of the plague or shall go outside the door, shall fall dead on the spot.' Isn't that what Padre Pio also said, speaking in the name of Christ: 'I will give you a sign to indicate the beginning of the great judgement: on a cold winter night I shall make thunder resound that will make the mountains shake. Then close your windows and do not look outside.'

The catastrophe will call a brutal halt to warfare and territorial ambitions. The spirit of conquest will vanish, stifled by terror. Men will be the playthings of a whole string of cataclysms: tidal waves, earthquakes, rains of stones and fire, deadly gases. Let us rather listen to Zephaniah, one of the 'minor' prophets in the Old Testament (1:15–18):

That day is a day of wrath,
a day of trouble and distress,
a day of wasteness and desolation,
a day of darkness and gloominess,
a day of clouds and thick darkness,
a day of the trumpet and alarm
against the fenced cities, and against the high
   towers.
And I will bring distress upon men,
that they shall walk like blind men,
because they have sinned against the Lord:
and their blood shall be poured out as dust,
and their flesh as the dung.
Neither their silver, nor their gold
shall be able to deliver them.

The prophecy of Prémol, so dramatic in style, is shocked by these new natural disasters: 'Come, O Lord! Your arm does not stop! Is not the fury of men enough for so many smoking ruins? Must the elements still serve your wrath? Stop, O Lord, stop! Your towns are destroying themselves.'

Indeed, this will be *coup de grâce* for most big cities, Paris in particular. Prince Hohenlohe, who was prone to prophetic visions, wrote in a letter dated 1828: 'Paris will be destroyed; the fire that fell on Sodom and Gomorrah will fall on her and to destroy her the sky will be one with the earth: Paris will be buried under a rain of sulphur and all that will be seen are precipices.'

'The capital will disappear in the flames,' said St Odile.

In 1846, the young shepherdess Mélanie Calvat, aged about 15, saw the Virgin at La Salette. Fifty years later, she went to Paris on the occasion of that anniversary. While walking along the quays, she suddenly had a vision which she told to a girlfriend who was with her: 'Do you see the Seine? If you knew how many people shall come there and be thrown in! And it is not so much who will be thrown in (there will certainly be some), but most of them will throw themselves in, driven mad, fleeing the fire suspended above the town! They will throw themselves in as if mad with terror, believing they could avoid the threatening fire in that way!'

*   *   *

Darkness will follow the flames. Actually the great cataclysm will plunge the Earth into a period of absolute darkness that will last, according to the Scriptures, for three days and three nights. In the same way, at the moment of Christ's death on the Cross, the sun was eclipsed and darkness lasted for three hours.

These three dark days will undoubtedly be due to the extraordinary mass of particles projected into the atmosphere. Unless, as I suggested earlier, they are the consequence of a change in the Earth's axis resulting from the impact of an asteroid on our planet. Our hemisphere will no longer see the sun, whereas the Asiatic and southern continents will grill under its pitiless rays. We find this shift of axis mentioned in Nostradamus:

> You will see soon and late make great change
> Horror, extremes and vindications
> As if the Moon led by its angel
> Heaven nears the inclinations.

However they come about and whatever their cause, the Three Days of the Lord will certainly be the cruellest ordeal of all. Will those who have survived the war and the planetary upsets be physically and morally strong enough to endure the agony that seems to teem down from heaven? Many of them will be unable to bear the cries of the dying resounding in the darkness.

What text better describes this moment when both the world and human reason are tottering than the *Voluspa*, a poem from Nordic mythology written around the ninth century?

> The mountains collapse,
> Men grope their way towards hell,
> And the heavens open,
> The sun grows dark,
> The land is lost in the sea,
> The stars vacillate in the heights of the sky . . .
> Brothers will kill brothers,
> Parents will destroy their own parents,
> The world will become perverse
> Man will collapse, stricken by man.

What advice do the sacred texts and the prophecies give us about what we should do? 'Go into the holes of the rock,' says the Old Testament, 'and into the caves of the earth.'

This is how the Abbess of Gandersheim, Sister Hroswitte, describes the conditions for survival: 'They will hollow out holes like moles, while the odour of death will spread through the air.'

In fact, it will be useless to try to escape. We read in the Revelation of St John that the only ones spared *in extremis* will be the 144,000 Just Men marked on their foreheads by the Lord before punishing the Earth. But in the meantime, in the indescribable chaos that will follow the fire and the night, the survivors (excepting the Just Men) will again be submitted to thousands of ordeals and punished according to their misdeeds. The Koran (Sura 23) says, 'Those who called our signs lies will be delivered to ignominious torture.' 'He that is far off shall die of the pestilence; and he that is near shall fall by the sword; and he that remaineth and is besieged shall die by the famine; thus will I accomplish my fury upon them,' says the Lord in the Book of Ezekiel (6:12). And Ezekiel continues (7:16 *et seq*):

> But they that escape of them shall escape, and shall be on the mountains like doves of the valleys, all of them mourning, every one for his iniquity. All hands shall be feeble, and all knees shall be weak as water . . . shame shall be on all faces, and baldness upon all their heads. They shall cast their silver in the streets, and their gold shall be removed . . . they shall not . . . fill their bowels.

The prophet Isaiah draws a similar picture: the end of the darkness does not put an end to man's torments:

> The inhabitants of the earth are burned and few men left. In the city is left desolation. When thus it shall be in the midst of the land among the people, there shall be as the shaking of an olive tree, and as the gleaning grapes when the vintage is done. But I said . . . woe unto me! the treacherous dealers have dealt treacherously; yea, the treacherous dealers have dealt very treacherously. Fear and the pit, and the snare are upon thee, O inhabitant of the earth . . . he who fleeth from the noise of the fear shall fall into the pit: and he who cometh up out of the midst of the pit shall be taken in the snare.

What kind of human beings will subsist on earth?
The kind described by the *Linga Purana* hardly
merits the name:

> People will kill each other in a fury. In the end
> there will remain here and there groups of people
> who will kill each other to steal from each other.
> Agitated and confused, they will abandon their
> wives and their houses. They will be without
> law, without shame, without love. They will live
> on roots and fruits, clad in bark, leaves and
> animal skins. They will no longer use money.
> They will be hungry and sick, and will know
> despair.

People will be reduced to cannibalism. I acquired this
horrible certainty from the visions impressed on me
by the Twenty-Four Elders before sending me to
Earth for my last incarnation. Unfortunately, I have
seen these images confirmed by Nostradamus. In an
already quoted quatrain, he tells us that famine will
be so universal that the babe will be torn from its
mother's breast and eaten. 'Men will become canni-
bals', we read in the Second Century, quatrain 75.

The prophecy of Prémol pushes the description of
this human decay to extremes: 'As corruption
increased, men turned into reptiles and bathed and
lived in these muddy waters.'

From then on, it is no longer a question of wars
about nationalities or religion. Everyone tries to survive in this new world that has neither faith nor law.
It is an epoch of physical and moral misery. This is
what Amos tells us: 'Behold the days come, saith the
Lord God, that I will send a famine in the land, not
a famine of bread, not a thirst for water, but of hearing the words of the Lord: And they shall
wander from sea to sea, and from the north even to

east . . . to seek the word of the Lord and shall not find it.'

* * *

Taking advantage of this total disarray, a man will arise, an apparently charismatic figure who will subjugate the whole Earth: the Antichrist!

In making that statement, I know that I am going against practically all the 'official' chronologies of the end of Time. My new idea will no doubt get me violently attacked by the adherents of eschatological orthodoxy. For they place the arrival of the Antichrist *after* that of the Great Monarch and the Great Pope, two beings who, as we shall see, will succeed in re-establishing harmony on earth.

I have never been able to adhere to this chronology, which I find completely illogical. It is difficult to see how the beneficent action of these two sovereigns, one temporal, the other spiritual, would open the door to the Evil One. If the Great Monarch succeeded in suppressing the disorder and encouraging more brotherly feelings on Earth, it is hard to understand him suddenly making room for the Antichrist's nefarious aims.

On the other hand, it is quite conceivable that a strong, even satanic figure, skilfully disguised at first as a 'saviour', would manage to impose himself on survivors regrouped into a few barbaric tribes. Those are souls among whom the Antichrist could easily reap a harvest. Quatrain 84 of Nostradamus's First Century seems to bring grist to my mill: 'The moon obscured in deep darkness (days of the Lord), his brother becomes rust-coloured, the great one (the Antichrist) long concealed in the gloom will plunge his blade in the bloody wound.'

*

When precisely will he come? Let us be cautious . . .
Should we follow the famous lines in quatrain 72 of
Nostradamus's Tenth Century, about which so
much has been written?

> In the year one thousand nine hundred and
>　ninety-nine
> and seven months a great king of terror
> will come from the skies.

This King of Terror could equally well mean the
comet of the Day of the Lord or the Antichrist. If we
follow my theory, the question is not so crucial, since
the two events are concomitant or nearly so. The year
1999 . . . The date seems very close today. Could the
end of Time come so quickly? Suffice it to note here
that by turning 1999 upside down and reversing it
we get 6661, the number of the Beast, opposed to
the divine One.

It is said that the Antichrist will be 33 at the
moment of his appearance—the same age as Christ
at his death. So the 'son of perdition' should be alive
at this moment.

In the course of my meditations, I have seen the face
of a young man living in London, who has surprised
important people by his 'magic' gifts. He is already
extending his psychic undertaking and his personal
fortune. The negative waves emanating from him are
the strongest I have ever felt. Is he no more than a sor-
cerer with extraordinary powers, or could he be the
Antichrist, already in ambush awaiting his hour? I
often reread and ask myself about the enigma in quatrain 76 of the Eighth Century of Nostradamus:

> More Macelin than King in England,
> born in an obscure place will win empire by force:
> coward without faith or law, he will bleed the land.
> His time is now so near that I sigh.

Once again and in spite of striking visions, I shall take good care neither to give the date of the end of our era nor to say that such and such a person is the Antichrist. I find it more interesting to ask what the true nature of the Antichrist will be—simple mortal or metaphysical image of evil? Above all, it seems to me that he must be the anti-Christ, the one who is opposed to Christ, rather than the Antechrist (the French word), he who comes before, who will precede the return of Christ. His real goal (not made known at the beginning of his reign) would be to eradicate Christ's message. He will be the ultimate personification of the Beast of Revelation, the symbolical monster on the lookout for any means to spread the word of Satan.

Risen from chaos, the Beast will play the angel for a time. The Antichrist will seduce the crowds, in whose eyes he will appear as a providential figure. According to the prophecies, he will put an end to the hostilities, pretending that he wants to save the earth. In reality, the 'Prince of Iniquity' will lead everyone who agrees to follow him to their ruin. And many will follow him, for he knows how to adopt every means of seduction. Disturbingly beautiful and formidably intelligent, he will soon get the upper hand by his charisma and become the Great Conciliator. winning the support of everyone, including the Believers. For this 'son of perdition', as St Paul calls him, will know how to present himself as a man of the Church and of prayer.

He will even perform miracles. The sibyl of Tibur, in the early centuries of Christianity, said of the Antichrist that 'by his magic sacrifices he will surprise the good faith of many who will see fire descending from heaven at the sound of his voice.' Indeed, he will appear to produce lightning, thunder and hail, to turn mountains over and change the course of rivers. He will pretend to heal the infirm, exorcise demons and sometimes bring the dead back to life.

He will be the quintessence of the false magi who are proliferating in our time. Knowing the success that these 'miracle-makers' achieve in the structured world of today, why be surprised if a being of exceptional ability, inspired by the Evil One, extends his power over the lost hordes emerging from the horrors of the Three Days of Darkness?

So his gifts will enable him to subjugate what remains of mankind and its leaders. The more alluring his sermons become, the larger his audience will be. A man of the Church, to be sure, but a Church consecrated to pleasure. 'You may do what you will,' St Hildegard makes him say. 'Give up fasting, it is enough that you loved me, I, who am your only God.'

Then his worshippers would be swallowed up in the rejection of all spirituality, the better to abandon themselves to the easy way of compliance. So will the Antichrist end up by imposing his social and political law. Firstly, he will put into practice the idea of a universal wage, the same for everybody, a programme that would obviously win him everybody's vote, considering the state of the planet.

Only then, once he has established his total power, will the Antichrist reveal his malice. People will realise that his sole aim was to establish his pernicious power over the world. At last he will appear as the Antichrist, that is to say the anti-generous, anti-love figure. 'He shall destroy wonderfully,' says Daniel (8:24–25), 'and shall prosper and practise, and shall destroy the mighty and the holy people . . . he shall cause craft to prosper in his hand; and he shall magnify himself in his heart.'

The Prince of Iniquity will find the means to maintain himself by using corruption, marvels and above all terror. All those who dare to raise their voice against him will be put to death.

In 954, the monk Adson wrote to Queen Gerberge, wife of the King of France, Louis IV d'Outremer: 'This fearful tribulation will last three and a half years, the forty-two months of the Apocalypse.'

*

Forty-two months, 1,260 days—that is also the time St John allots to the Two Witnesses to tread under foot the holy city in order to oppose the power of the Beast. These two prophets are the reincarnations of Enoch and Elijah, the patriarch and the prophet who share the experience of having been taken up into heaven without having died. Enoch is endowed with colossal force, whereas Elijah is a young man irradiating light.

The two witnesses will rise up against the Antichrist, but without at first conquering him. They will be put to death in Rome, reconstructed by the Antichrist who will have made it the seat of his planetary domination. Their bodies will be exposed for everyone to look at.

But with this last crime, the Prince of Iniquity will sign his death warrant. This is how St Hildegard relates his death:

> When the son of perdition shall have accomplished all his aims, he will assemble his followers and tell them that he wishes to ascend to heaven. At the very moment of this ascension, a flash of lightning will strike him and cause his death. In addition, the mountain to which he had repaired to effect his ascension will be instantly covered by a cloud that will spread an insupportable odour of corruption, all of which, at the sight of his body covered with decay, will open the eyes of a great number of people and make them realise their miserable error.

Is the (true) miracle that signals the destruction of the Antichrist a sign of divine pity? Undoubtedly. Mankind seems to have reached the limits of ignominy and suffering, but also of punishment. And the Just Men survive. The 144,000 Just Men of the Revelation of St John (or more, or less, we shall see; that will depend on each one of us). In their case, God decides to put an end to the enormous punishment. Remember the Gospel according to St Matthew (24:22): 'And except those days should be shortened, there should no flesh be saved: but for the elect's sake those days shall be shortened.'

*

These terrible tribulations that I have just recalled should open on 'a new heaven and a new earth'. As epigraph to this chapter, I quoted this line by Nostradamus: 'When the fishing boat shall be lost . . .' The reference is obvious. For at the end of all these ordeals, it is the age of Pisces that will come to an end. 'There shall be no more sorrow, nor crying, neither shall there be any more pain,' St John rejoices at the end of Revelation, 'for the former things are passed away.'

Chapter 7

FROM ONE ERA TO ANOTHER ...

Those whose foreheads will be marked

And ye shall hear of wars and rumours of wars: see that ye be not troubled: for all these things must come to pass.

Gospel according to St Matthew

After the unleashing of the storm a fine soothing rain will sprinkle the Earth. The trumpets and the celestial uproar will give way to a peaceful silence. The great apocalyptic tribulations will finally be ended, thanks to God. The Antichrist overthrown, the Beast will be hurled 'into a lake of fire burning with brimstone', St John tells us, and Satan will be chained up.

At first the death of the Antichrist will throw the crowds into great confusion: the collapse of the political system and the false morality that he erected will leave a painful void.

But this last ordeal will be of short duration. For then will appear a figure who has genuinely come to save. He is the Great Monarch mentioned by all the 'cyclologies' of the end of Time, although they place his arrival before that of the Antichrist for some strange reason. I have already put forward the reasons why I cannot support that thesis: in my opinion, the Antichrist could not follow the two great figures who will restore the Spirit of God to Earth: Pontifex Maximus and the Great Monarch.

Traditional imagery associates this sovereign with the colour white, which marks both the end of the night and the birth of day. Symbolising death as

well as renewal, white is *par excellence* the colour
of transition. The reign of this renowned monarch
closes the age of Pisces and opens the age of
Aquarius.

In the fourteenth century blessed Raban Maur,
archbishop of Mainz, councillor of Louis le Preux,
announced the arrival of this sovereign: 'Towards
the end of Time a descendant of the French kings
will establish his reign over everything which was
once the Roman Empire: he will be the greatest and
the last of all the kings . . .' You will find an echo of
this prophecy in St Remi, Archbishop of Rheims,
who says that the Great King 'will arrive as if by a
miracle, and that he will be of blood of the old stock
("cape" in French).'

Does this mean that he will be a descendant of the
kings of France, of the Capetians in particular? That
is the interpretation put on it by many scholars. Personally, I am not so sure. This theory concentrates
too much on the idea of a royalist restoration to win
my support. On the other hand, I am extremely interested in the idea of descent: the Great Monarch is
presented as the heir to a secular, even millenary
tradition. Moreover, was not Raban Maur only repeating what St Augustine (354–430) had written long
before him? One can go even farther back, because
before evoking the personality of the Great Monarch,
St Augustine, the famous bishop of Hippo, himself indicated that he was only handing on a far
older tradition: 'Some of our doctors say that a
French king will possess the Roman Empire one
day . . .'

For Nostradamus, on the other hand, the Sovereign will come from the Orient. But above all, the
sage of Salon-de-Provence suggests that his famous
heritage will be of an esoteric nature (Tenth Century,
quatrain 75):

The one so long awaited will never come back
to Europe. He will appear in Asia,
one of the league issued from great Hermes,
he will grow greater than all the Kings of the East.

The Hermes here in question is obviously Hermes Trismegistus, the author of *Corpus Hermeticum*, a collection of treatises which combines the Egyptian science with Neoplatonic philosophy, asserting that the cosmos is a living being and that man is an integral part of it. So the Great Monarch would belong to the long line of heirs to the esoteric Tradition.

I am convinced that in spite of the destruction caused by the apocalyptic strife, the famous secrets of the Atlanteans, the depositories of which were Egypt and Mesopotamia, will never completely disappear. Far from it! The new era which will begin after the death of the Antichrist will draw its genius from the rediscovery of this sacred Knowledge. That is also what the *Voluspa*, the great cosmological text of the Nordic peoples, prophesies: 'At the heart of the greenery, men will rediscover the gold tablets, marvellous tablets which their ancestors had possessed in the earliest days . . .' Whether he comes from Europe or the Orient, the Great Monarch will be first and foremost a great Initiate.

Enlightened by this primal knowledge, he will prove to be an exemplary sovereign. The prophecy of Prémol describes his accession to glory as follows: 'And I saw a remarkable young man mounted on a lion coming from the Orient: he held a flaming sword in his hand and the Cock sang before him. And at his passage, all the peoples bowed.' The lion is the symbol of sovereign power, but also of wisdom and justice. And the luminous blade suggests the conquest of Knowledge rather than martial ardour.

For even if he is a fighting man, the Great Monarch

will be above all the redeemer and rallier of all the survivors. And his reign will encourage the actions of another figure foretold by the prophecies: Pontifex Maximus, the Great Pope. So it is true that the apocalyptic tribulations will be followed by a reconciliation between the temporal and the spiritual. If the peoples bowed before the Great Monarch as they did, says the prophecy of Prémol, it is because 'the Spirit of God was in him. He came on the ruins of Sion, and he put his hand in the Pontiff's hand.' 'The two united heart and soul will make the reformation of the world triumph', rejoices St Caesarius.

Hold on, though! This is not a case of dishonourable collusion between the Army and the Church, by which the privileged few enslaved the people for so long! Our ancient kings of France give a very poor idea of the infallible guide represented in the Great Monarch, in the same way that the popes of the Catholic Church are only painful caricatures of the future Pontifex Maximus.

Indeed, under the impulse of the latter, renaissant humanity will take part in a genuine restoration of the Church. A new religion will see the light of day, undoubtedly one closer to original Christianity. There will be an end to all the religiosity and the dogmas imposed on the faithful; forgotten will be all the Vaticanesque pomp which openly flouts the vow of austerity taken by the early Christians! The Great Pope will demonstrate his humility. Christ walked barefoot and possessed only a homespun robe: he did not wear a single gold jewel and ate out of gourds or earthenware dishes. In the same way, when the Church of Aquarius comes, simplicity will finally drive out ostentation.

This extraordinary rejuvenation of Christianity was prophesied in the nineteenth century by Joseph de Maistre: 'It is not a question of a modernisation of the Church, but of a new form of the eternal religion which will be to Christianity what the latter is to Judaism.' A change of era implies a change of religion . . . After Aries, Pisces; after Pisces, Aquarius.

Traditionally, the sign of Aquarius is represented by a man holding an amphora on his shoulder or under his arm. We meet this symbol in the Gospel according to St Luke (22:10): 'There shall a man meet you, bearing a pitcher of water, follow him,' Christ tells the Apostles who ask him where they should prepare the Passover meal, which will also be their last meal before the arrest and crucifixion of Jesus. Now the Passover (Easter) is the feast to commemorate the Jews' exodus from Egypt. Before the exterminating plague struck the land of the Pharaohs, the Hebrews had sacrificed the Lamb, collected its blood and marked the lintels of their doors so that the Lord would spare their houses. Passover is synonymous with a passage through suffering, that of the Hebrews from slavery to freedom, that of Christ from death to resurrection. Luke's mention of the pitcher-bearer guiding the Apostles towards the paschal feast can equally well serve as a parable for the future: could it not also stand for the passage of the chosen in the age of Aquarius, in the midst of the apocalyptic torments?

'The earth shall be filled with peace as a receptacle may be filled with water,' the Islamic Tradition tells us; 'there will be universal concord.' Is not this receptacle full of water the pitcher of Aquarius once again?

Christianity's long-stifled ecumenic vocation will develop to the full. The Pontifex Maximus will perform the miracle of gathering all the religions together. 'There shall be one fold, and one shepherd,' says John (10:16). The same Spirit of God will be present in all men: 'I will pour out of my spirit upon all flesh,' we read in the Acts of the Apostles (2:17). 'It shall come to pass that . . . all flesh come to worship before me,' Isaiah prophesies (66:23). That will be the advent of the Church of universal love . . .

*

Alliance without clashes between the civilian and religious parties, fusion of the different religions. Then mankind will enter the Millennium, a cycle of peace and spirituality. The word Millennium does not necessarily designate a thousand years, as some people claim, but a long and glorious period of plenitude which covers the age of Aquarius, during which Satan will stay in chains.

Mankind will have risen to the Fourth Vibratory Plane. That does not imply that we shall be wholly spiritual: it means that we shall have reached a stage in evolution which will enable us better to control the necessary balance between rationality and spirituality, between matter and spirit. The civilisation of Aquarius will function according to a new way of thinking. Our relations with others and with the world will be changed.

After the passage of the apocalyptic hurricane, after the blackest and vilest thoughts have been purged out, Nature will be as if in its virgin state again. It will be reconciled with Science which will no longer be the (sometimes) destructive despot of the planet that we know. After the rediscovery of the Atlantean secrets, scientists will place themselves entirely in the service of mankind, with absolute respect for our mother Gaia. It will not be a question of a return to a primitive age: on the contrary, the Millennium will see a highly developed civilisation flourish, but one whose 'gentle' technologies will not attack the ecosystem.

As for our relations with others, they will evolve in the same way. Aquarius is the sign of fluidity, and of fraternity. The moral imperatives that are still distant ideals for us ('Love thy neighbour as thyself') will seem to be perfectly natural modes of behaviour. Consideration for the human person, understanding of individual aspirations, a feeling of belonging to a close-knit community, mutual aid—such will be the values ruling the Fourth Vibratory Plane. This is how Isaiah evoked this idyllic period (65:25): 'The wolf and the lamb shall feed together, and the lion shall eat straw like the bullock: and dust shall be the serpent's meat. They shall not hurt nor destroy in all my holy mountain.'

As for the organisation of this Aquarian society and what it will look like, we can still only dream. In my meditations, I have seen white marble monuments, I have seen streets paved with gold (for gold will no longer have any market value), I have seen people, men and women, wearing the same simple and comfortable tunics. Parnassian, Edenlike images such as are found in all the 'cyclologies' and are especially reminiscent of the new Jerusalem of Revelation:

> And the foundations of the city were garnished with all manner of precious stones. The first foundation was jasper; the second, sapphire, the third, a chalcedony; the fourth, an emerald; the fifth, sardonyx; the sixth, a sardius; the seventh, chrysolite; the eighth, beryl; the ninth, a topaz; the tenth, a chrysophrasus; the eleventh, a jacint; the twelfth, an amethyst. And the twelve gates were twelve pearls; every several gate was of one pearl: and the street of the city was pure gold, as it were transparent glass.

*

From that time on mankind will continue its course. Undoubtedly it will experience other cycles, other precessional years. In a future so remote that we can barely make it out, will come the Parousia, Christ's glorious second coming, so often foretold in the

Gospels. Foretold and longed for. 'Come, Lord Jesus!' we read in the last lines of Revelation.

In my opinion, the Parousia will not be the return of Jesus 'pure and simple'. For it must contain progression, evolution, the pathway towards God. The first men were polytheists: Moses (to choose a landmark) invented the monotheistic religion. In olden days, the Gods were represented by natural elements or animals. The Hebraic religion made of them one God who could no longer be named nor described without committing sacrilege. 'I am that I am', was all the Lord said. The primitive God was vindictive: later he made a covenant with men. The age of Aquarius and the Millennium will represent a new stage in which man will possess the sacred Knowledge and be able to find the ways to the Divine. The Parousia will be the final apotheosis, fusion with celestial Light, accession to the Seventh Vibratory Plane.

Then will come the end of the world as we know it. The moment when 'the heaven departed as a scroll when it is rolled together', John of Patmos tells us. After the Big Bang the Bang Big must come. 'I am Alpha and Omega,' says the Lord in Revelation. This ultimate Apocalypse will be the Supreme Revelation, when all the cosmic energies will blend with the unique All.

*   *   *

But it is very hard for us to imagine the Parousia, since we even find the advent of an enlightened Great Monarch and a Sovereign Pontiff with an ecumenical vocation almost impossible to visualise! How can we expect a universal and naturally fraternal civilisation when we see the brutality of dictatorial regimes and the cynicism of our so-called democracies spreading day by day? Democracies, for example, which do not hesitate to inject contaminated blood into the veins of their citizens* or deliberately use humanitarian cover to disguise military interventions with strategic or purely financial goals.

What an incredible gulf separates us from the reconciliations of the age of Aquarius as we have just described it! What shock, what extraordinary cataclysm must we endure for such a revolution of thought to take place and for the new golden age to see the light of day? For if we refuse to take the necessary measures to ensure a smooth transition, there will only be one solution left: our civilisation will come to an abrupt end.

We should not forget that this passage to the age of Aquarius will take place whether we like it or not. It is recorded in the Cosmos. In one or two decades, we shall change the month in the precessional year, and the fisher of fish will lay down his net so that the young man representing Aquarius can arise. The precise moment is difficult to calculate. Let us say the astronomic turning-point lies between 2005 and 2030. At all events, the change is not a wish, but an unavoidable reality which will not await our pleasure.

The problem is that the farther mankind deviates from the path it ought to take, the more brutal will be the return imposed on it. The more we ignore Gaia's appeals to change the Vibratory Plane, the greater the danger that we will not be able to make the great leap allowing us to enter the new age in safety.

*

* Cf. Nostradamus, Fifth Century, quatrain 96:

The rose on the middle of the great world,
because of new facts, public blood is spread.
To tell the truth, mouths will stay shut,
when in time of need, what is awaited arrives late.

What augurs ill for our chances is the general apathy I have already mentioned, in which many individuals seem to find solace. Because they benefit by the status quo or because any change would cost them dear, some even deny that there is anything urgent about the situation. These disbelievers prefer to deride the prophesies. They slap their thighs and say: 'None of that will happen!' Peter has already warned us in his Second Epistle (3:3–7):

> Knowing this first, that there shall come in the last days scoffers, walking after their own lusts, and saying, where is the promise of his coming? for since the fathers fell asleep, all things continue as they were from the beginning of the creation. For this they willingly are ignorant of, that by the word of God the heavens were of old, and the earth standing out of the water and in the water: whereby the world that then was, being overflowed with water, perished: But the heavens and the earth, which are now, by the same word are kept in store, reserved unto fire against the day of judgement and perdition of ungodly men.

The last-named, ignoring all the warnings, are content to live from day to day, and take what they can. Never mind about tomorrow: '*Après nous le Deluge!*' 'They say: there is no other life but the present life'; says the Koran in Sura 45. But when the day comes, they will perish, 'because they have taken the signs of God as an object for their mockery, and the life of the world has dazzled them.'

Others will not lift their little finger because they are terrified. They note how the dangers are increasing everywhere, but they react badly. They retreat, ready to defend their little corner tooth and nail. They cling on to their material possessions as if they expected to take them into the tomb. Fear is usually a wretched counsellor. Especially since, in these 'Reduced Times', our instincts have a tendency to run amok and drag us in dangerous directions. So the fearful are perfectly aware of the danger, but they do not realise that, panicking as they do, they emit waves of anguish which amplify even more the negative 'Watcher' vibrations weighing on our Blue Planet. They identify themselves with the aggressiveness and folly which are in a fair way to precipitate them, even more surely, towards catastrophe.

One last cause of apathy in the face of emergency: resignation. In drawing a black picture (but one which I feel is perfectly accurate) of the planetary situation, by enumerating the terrible torments that may await us, I know that I run the risk of plunging some people into a form of 'despair', in the etymological sense of 'without hope.' Have they forgotten the saying, while there's life, there's hope? Undoubtedly, for they have lost the will to fight back.

And this giving up is exactly what I am trying to fight against today! I am not brandishing the catalogue of apocalyptic tribulations like a preacher seeking to terrorise his sheep into becoming a respectful and docile flock. But I am aware that, having reached this point of reflection on the Apocalypse, some will be tempted to resign themselves to their fate, overcome by their impotence in the face of the possible scope of a planetary catastrophe, among other disasters. Now that would be to commit an error on a colossal scale! At the very moment when it ought to be fully aware of the problem of its survival, mankind might turn into an enormous herd of cattle allowing itself to be led to the slaughter-house.

*   *   *

Thoughtlessness, catalepsy or capitulation . . . All these unpardonable attitudes neglect one vital fact:

we are not merely witnesses to this end of civilisation, we are actors in it as well! Each one of us is
a part of the world, intrinsically bound to it, and by
no means can we shed our responsibility for it. The
fate of mankind is not something totally abstract
that we should leave in the hands of a few politicians
for whom electoral deadlines are unfortunately far
more pressing than those of eschatology. We can still
influence our destiny at the individual and collective
level.

For emergency or not, we still preserve our freedom
of choice untouched. At every moment in our lives,
even when confronted with the worst difficulties, we
still have the possibility of making a choice. Remember what I said about the symbolism of Adam and
Eve's apple . . . Today we can opt for artificial para-
dises, for bogus occultism or for lucidity and positive
action. Our freedom of choice still offers us the possibility of going back on our decisions and correcting
our civilisation's suicidal tendencies.

But what are we to do? The first necessity, is . . .
to pray. Luke (21:36) presses us to do so: 'Watch ye
therefore, and pray ye always, that ye may be
accounted worthy to escape all these things that
shall come to pass.'

For about two centuries, the most pressing exhortations have come from the Virgin. 'Pray, but pray constantly!' Mary demanded at the time of her apparition
at Beauraing, a small village in Belgium, in 1933.
'People pray so little!' she cried in distress at San
Damiano in 1965. 'If they do not pray, the scourges
will come in great numbers and be very strong.'

But already I hear the mockers: what can a prayer
do to save the world? It is important to explain that
prayer does not mean mumbling a sequence of words
learnt by heart. It is not a question of mechanically
reciting one's rosary: an *Our Father* for the large
beads, a *Hail Mary* for the small ones. For me, prayer

constitutes an opening of consciousness, it is a form of listening in to the world and to others. To pray is to place oneself in a state of pure generosity, of the gratuitous gift of self. It is a dilatation, a relaxation, a joyous submission to the divine munificence. To pray is to enlarge one's perception of reality, to cease shutting oneself up in an impoverishing egoism in order to go against all those who suffer.

Ultimately, prayer is calling on the All, and so making contact with that cosmic energy which runs through all things. I live permanently with the sensation that the world surrounding me and the accumulation of cells that forms me have been deliberately created by an extraordinary thought, which is simultaneously external and internal to me, but which is above all a thought of love. During meditation, I express to this creative power my awareness that I owe my existence to it. I become conscious of the fact that all the beings on this planet are of the same stuff as myself, that we are like the drops of water that form the ocean. Naturally I am 'obliged' to love anyone who meets me, since our origin and our substance are identical.

I have always distrusted people who preach loud and long the 'right to difference'. No, we are not different, we are alike, without distinction of age, class or race. The other is always another myself. The 'right to difference' undoubtedly sets out with the best of intentions, but let us not forget that it is also in the name of that difference that we keep others at arm's length, that racism and hate of all kinds are fed. Is it not also in the name of difference that we justify the misery, the ghettos, ethnic Balkanisation, the subjection of women and the condemnation of mixed marriages?

On the other hand, to be in a state of prayer is to go towards the other. It is a constant attitude, expressed not solely by adopting bombastic positions, but in the simplest gestures in life: a door always open, equal consideration given to everyone, humble or powerful, a welcoming smile for the stranger, a curiosity ever on the alert, a hand offered to a crying child. This love that created us, it must flower like an aura, reflect all around us. Life is a joy whose vibrations I feel everywhere. And the more I give, the more I receive.

Looked at in this way, meditation is never an egoistic art. To pray is to pray for humanity, for others, and so (but lastly) for oneself. It is to create a positive 'watching' vibration that chases the darkness away. If all the inhabitants of the planet prayed in this way, together, for a whole day, I wager the Earth could be saved. All the wars, all the catastrophes of which we have spoken, would be avoided or reduced to a few minor disturbances. You are still sceptical? And yet, how could men take up arms against each other, if they all combined to become genuinely aware of their total osmosis? But don't let's dream. Are men prepared for this universal communion? Nevertheless, the words of the Virgin at the time of her appearance at Kerizinen in Brittany in 1948 leave us a gleam of hope: 'Soon, when historians look for the event that changed the face of the world, that brought it peace and prosperity, they will find out that it was not a battle, but a prayer.'

This call for a profoundly mystical, fervent prayer, however, does not mean that we must give up everything to immerse ourselves completely in a strictly meditative life. After being too concerned with material goods, we should only be exchanging one imbalance for another. For centuries we have favoured the material to the detriment of the spiritual, the rational to the detriment of the feeling side. This has led to the exploitation of Nature, to the frenzied cult of the body, to the desire for possession. Today it is imperative for us to change direction— taking care, however, not to change direction towards the spiritual too suddenly. We should leave one excess for another and then we should become an easy prey for all the gurus and false prophets whose disastrous activities we have already denounced.

Uncontrolled mysticisms often beget a pernicious and above all ineffectual pride. Let us keep our feet on the ground, with our imperatives as human beings, our minimum of materiality to manage. It is not a matter, for example, of devoting oneself entirely to others, but more simply of being always ready to give. The rich will not be automatically excluded from the number of Just Men, provided that, 'in their wealth, there is a part for the beggar and for the unfortunate' (the Koran, Sura 21).

As I have already said, what we should force ourselves to do is to re-establish the equilibrium between materiality and spirituality, between the body and the soul. For we shall be unable to rise to the Fourth Vibratory Plane of the age of Aquarius without a harmonious increase in these two complementary principles.

*

As for the great upheavals that will accompany the passage from one era to another, once again their scale is a matter about which we have free choice. Nothing is lost and, in the absence of a universal prayer that could change everything as if by a 'miracle' (for it would be one), I see reasons for hope on all sides. Individuals and governments have become aware that a change of behaviour is needed. Both parties are taking the first steps and making an effort to lower their barriers in favour of a certain measure of generosity. True, there are always grumblers to criticise or gibe at the least initiative! Recently, for example, there has been much emphasis on the perverse effects of the 'charity show'; the fact that this phenonemon revealed a formidable burst of altruism was forgotten.

Here and there, I learn that prayer groups are forming. People meet to pray for others, for sick people near and far, for friends or strangers, and also for the world's health. That has been done since the dawn of time in convents and monasteries, but is it not a hopeful sign to see 'civilians', people 'of the century', practise such collective prayer in their turn?

At government level, too, just look at the progress that has been made in the last ten or twenty years! The scientists' and ecologists' cries of alarm have finally been heard by politicians and diplomats. From protocol to conference and various conventions, there is a gradual passage from declarations of intent to concrete measures in the fight against pollution or the reduction of armaments. To be sure, we are attacking the ill late in the day and the success of the cure cannot be guaranteed, but at least a treatment has been started. We have understood that any other attitude would lead inevitably to destruction. Scholars, intellectuals and the clergy are striving to formulate a new ethic which would no longer be founded on the exploitation of Nature or humans. They are settling to the formidable task of reconciling the ecology, in the broadest sense of the word, with the necessary technological development.

And in the field of religion we see meetings (still timid, true, but promising) between the leaders of different religious persuasions. I also rediscovered the expansion that is being achieved by prayer in the movement for global advancement, which is growing in spite of national resistance. Thus more and more people are ready to assert that their country is the Earth—something that a conference of Heads of State at The Hague in 1989 summed up by a striking piece of unintentional humour: 'As the problems are planetary, their solutions can only be conceived at world level.' The sociologist Edgar Morin, for his part, emphasises that we have reached 'the historic moment when the fundamental exigency of a unity of the human species is imposing itself . . . If mankind does not succeed in realising this unity, it will certainly run the risk of self-destruction.'

Everywhere I hear that one of the founding principles of the secret doctrine, namely that the world is one, the part is in the whole and the whole in the part, is being accepted as a new truth. This attitude has some vital consequences. It means in effect that everything must be considered as interrelated. Henceforth we know that there is no longer an 'elsewhere'. For example, we can no longer get rid of our nuclear or chemical waste among our neighbours, for this 'elsewhere' is still among us.

Such an idea illuminates relations between rich and poor countries from a new angle. The former begin to understand that they cannot continue to exploit the latter without risking a serious backfire: destabilising migrations, social explosion, ravaging of the ecological heritage, warlike intentions. Henceforth, heads of state and international organisations can establish a direct link between development and peace. One more affirmation of the positive nature of expansion and dilatation . . .

*

So we see a new way of thinking and new ways of behaving appearing in every sphere and at all levels. Nevertheless, we must not shout victory too soon. The dangers I have enumerated throughout this book are too weighty to be swept away so quickly. All the more so as the growing awareness is still far from being universal or sincere. One example among others: a few years ago, the United Nations took the decision to invite each member country to devote one per cent of its gross national product to aid for the countries of the Third World. Up to the present, this decision has not been respected by a single State, with the exception of Sweden.

So we should beware of a too angelical optimism. Our civilisation has undoubtedly swung too far to the negative side for us to expect a gentle passage into the age of Aquarius. Let us simply say, and please forgive the triviality of the remark, that we can still do much to limit the damage.

Having said that, what attitude is left for us to adopt as individuals, faced with damage of major or minor importance? Acceptance (which does not mean resignation) seems to me the only solution. 'Place yourselves under the invocation of my Mother,' says Christ, through the mouth of Padre Pio. 'Whatever you may see or hear, do not despair . . . Have no doubt about your deliverance! I will guard you from all danger if you have trust in My Love.' Once each of us has made every possible effort to achieve amelioration, altruism, in short elevation to a higher plane, what else can we do but entrust ourselves to the divine will?

The Revelation of St John tells us that only those marked on their foreheads will be saved. The same idea appears in the Gospel according to St Luke (17: 33–35): 'Whosoever shall seek to save his life shall lose it; and whosoever shall lose his life, shall preserve it. I tell you, in that night there shall be two men in one bed; the one shall be taken, and the other shall be left. Two women shall be grinding together; one shall be taken, and the other shall be left' So let us give ourselves every chance to figure among those who will be marked with divine mercy. And if we lack the greatness, or simply the strength, to mend our ways, if we cannot 'choose', of our own free will, this narrow and difficult but saintly path, let us simply choose God! The best use we can make of our free choice is what I call 'letting go': 'Thy will be done!' say our prayers. It is by this total abandonment to the flux of divine energy that we shall have a chance of belonging to the Just Men saved from the chaos and the ordeals. How many will there be? 144,000, according to the Revelation of St John. But it depends entirely on us to make them more numerous. For in these Reduced Times, we are offered a remarkable opportunity: the power of the cosmic vibrations at this end of the Kali Yuga act as an accelerator of time. People are able to develop their awareness much quicker than before. The quest for the Knowledge which often took a whole lifetime, and even several, can take place today in the form of an almost instantaneous revelation. 'Your sons and your daughters shall prophesy,' we read in the Bible, 'your old men shall dream dreams, your young men shall see visions.'

The Elect will be those who knew how to throw a bridge towards this suprasensible world. The mark on the forehead which distinguishes them, according to St John, is it not precisely the sixth chakra of Hindu tradition? This subtle centre is the place of passage of cosmic energy 'with the thousand-petalled lotus', situated at the top of the head and the opening of which corresponds to the revelation of the universal consciousness. Thus the Just Men will not be those who have followed to the letter a rigid moral code, enacted by men. They are those who have attained a level of spirituality enabling them to perceive the Divinity in all things, those for whom prayer is no longer only a word, but an *act* of love.

The more numerous the people to reach this stage, the more the apocalyptic torments will be diminished. We must remember that God is not an avenging force which will take a sadistic or puerile pleasure in destroying his Creation. His punishment will not exceed our faults. Better still, as we have said, He will shorten our sufferings out of pity for the Just Men, so the apocalyptic tribulations will have as much violence as we wish to give them! Because he is the simple catalyser of our negative energies, the Antichrist will have only the power he can draw from us. Let us act so as to limit his powers as much as possible, and this end of a cycle will take place in the best conditions. The planetary catastrophes could change into minor upsets.

On the scale of man's History the Apocalypse is only a stage, and not the Great Punishment. I refuse to believe that God created the world to lead it to the impasse of destruction or to satisfy a desire for vengeance. The Lord is Pity. And the Apocalypse is a Revelation: that of the development of man and his long ascent towards the light. Every time they become unaware of this truth people are in danger of seeing themselves brutally called to order. Since its origins, humanity has undertaken a long voyage that we have no right to interrupt before the final flowering. 'I am Alpha and Omega,' says the Lord at the end of St John's prophetic book, 'the beginning and the end, the first and the last. Blessed are they that do his commandments that they may have right to the tree of life, and may enter through the gates into the city.'

The essential thing is to persuade oneself that the worst has never won. And if humanity takes itself in hand in time (as a matter of absolute urgency) and manages to enter the age of Aquarius without a universal catastrophe, then it will have shown itself worthy of its name and of its Creator!

BIBLIOGRAPHY

Anthologie de la Poésie nordique ancienne, translated by Renauld-Kranz, Unesco-Gallimard, Paris, 1964.

D'ARES, Jacques, *Encyclopédie de l'ésoterisme*, Editions du Jour, J.-P. Delarge. *Atlantis*, No. 364, Winter 1991, 'Où en sommes-nous de la fin des temps?'

AUCLAIR, Raoul, *la Fin des temps, le nouveau livre des cycles*, Librairie Fayard, 1973.

——*Kerizinen, apparitions en Bretagne*, Nouvelles Editions latines, Paris, 1968.

BELLECOUR, Elizabeth, *Nostradamus trahi*, suivi du texte original et complet des dix centuries, Editions Robert Laffont, 1981.

BERLITZ, Charles, *Atlantis, the last continent revealed*, Macmillan, London, 1984.

BOEHME, Jacob, *Mysterium Magnum*, Aubier-Montaigne, Paris, 1978.

BOKHARI, El, *les Traditions islamiques*, translated by O. Houdas, Paris, 1914.

BRICON, Edouard, *Recueil des prédictions depuis le seizième siècle jusqu'à la consommation des temps*, Librairie catholique Edouard Bricon, Paris, 1830.

CARNAC, Pierre, *Le Monde commence à Bimini*, Editions Robert Laffont, 1973.

——*Prophéties et prophètes de tous les temps*, Editions Pygmalion, Paris, 1991.

CERBELAUD-SALAGNAC, Georges, *Fatima et notre temps*, Editions France-Empire, 1967.

CHARPENTIER, Josane, *le Livre de Prophéties*, Editions Astra, Paris, 1982.

CHARROUX, Robert, *One Hundred Thousand Years of Man's Unknown History*, translated by Lowell Blair, Sphere Books, London, 1981.

COLIN-SIMARD, Annette, *les Apparitions de la Vierge*, Librairie Fayard, Paris, 1981.

DHORME, Edouard, *les Religions de Babylonie et d'Assyrie*, Paris, 1949.

DORESSE, J., *The Secret Books of the Egyptian Gnostics, an introduction to the gnostic manuscripts discovered at Chenoboskion*, Inner Traditions International, 1986.

DUMEZIL, Georges, *les Dieux indo-européens*, PUF, 1957.

ELIADE, Mircea, *The Myth of the Eternal Return*, Arkana, London, 1989.

——*la Nostalgie des origines*, Gallimard, Paris, 1971.

——*Patterns in Comparative Religion*, Sheed & Ward, London, 1958.

FERRY, Luc, *le Nouvel ordre écologique*, Editions Grasset & Fasquelle, 1992.

FESTUGIERES, A. J., *le Révélation de Hermès Trismégiste*, Les Belles Lettres, Paris, 1983.

FROSSARD, André, *le Parti de Dieu, Lettre aux Evêques*, Librairie Fayard, 1992.

GABRIEL, Jean, *Presence de la Très Sainte Vierge à San Damiano*, Nouvelles Editions latines, 1975.

GIEBEL, Josef, *Prophéties face à la science*, Editions Sand, 1983.

The Glorious Koran, bilingual edition with English translation by Marmaduke Pickthall, Allen & Unwin, London, 1976.

GOLDSMITH, Edward, and HILDYARD, Nicholas (eds), *The Earth Report, monitoring the battle for our environment*, Mitchell Beazley, London, 1988.

GRAVELAINE, Joëlle de, *Prédictions et Prophéties*, Librairie Hachette, Paris, 1965.

GUENON, René, *Formes traditionnelles et cycles cosmiques*, Gallimard, 1970.

——*Introduction générale à l'étude des doctrines hindoues*, Vega, 1976.

The Holy Bible, Authorised Version (The King James Bible).

HUTIN, Serge, *les Civilisations inconnues*, Arthème Fayard, 1961.

KOECHLIN de BIZEMONT, Dorothée, *Prophéties d'Edgar Cayce*, Editions du Rocher, Monaco, 1989.

KRAMER, S. N., *History Begins at Sumer*, second edition, Thames & Hudson, London, 1961.

KRAVELIC, S., *les Apparitions de Mejdugorje*, Paris, 1988.

LACARRIERE, Jacques, *En suivant les dieux*, Philippe Lebaud Editeur, 1984.

LE COUR, Paul, *l'Ere du Verseau*, Dervy-Livres, Paris, 1980.

LE COUR, Paul, D'ARES, Jacques, and TODERICIU, Doru, *l'Atlantide atlantique*, Atlantis, 1971.

La légende immémoriale du dieu Shiva, le Shiva-Purana, translated from the Sanskrit by Tara Michaël, Editions Gallimard, Paris, 1991.

LE HIDEC, Max, *les Secrets de La Salette*, Nouvelles Editions latines, 1969.

LIPOVETSKY, Gilles, *l'Ere du vide, Essais sur l'individualisme contemporain*, Editions Gallimard, Paris, 1985.

MAXENCE, Jean-Luc, *la Mystérieuse prophétie de saint Malachie*, Oswald, 1979.

MURAISE, Eric, *Histoire et légende du grand monarque*, Albin Michel, 1976.

NIEL, Fernand, *la Civilisation des mégalithes*, Plon, 1970.

NOSTRADAMUS, *The Prophecies*, bilingual edition edited and with English translation by Erika Cheetham, Corgi, 1975.

PHAURE, Jean, *la Cycle de l'Humanité Adamique*, Dervy-Livres, Paris, 1988.

PLATO, *Timaeus* and *Critias*, translated by H. D. P. Lee, Penguin Books, Harmondsworth, 1971.

POCHAN, André, *l'Enigme de la grand pyramide*, Laffont, 1971.

ROSTAND, Jean, *Inquiétudes d'un biologiste*, Stock, 1967.

ROUDENE, Alex, *le Prophéties, vérité ou mensonges?*, Les Editions de l'Athanor, Paris, 1976.

SANCHEZ-VENTURA Y PASCUAL, F., *Marie annonce la fin des temps*, Nouvelles Editions latines, 1969.

Science et Avenir, No. 584, October 1992, '26 Septembre 2000, la collision? Les fins du monde'.